ABOUT THE AUTHOR

A veteran mountain biker, Tim Woodcock hit the dirt in the wake of his two teenage sons, and hasn't looked back since - much to the dismay of his long-suffering partner and bike-widow, Kay. She's never forgiven him since their youngest son, now three, uttered his first word: 'Bike'. On his first Polaris Challenge Tim managed an impressive sixth place in his category; but Tim claims he is not obsessive about mountain biking. He is a respected journalist and a fine photographer. His work often appears in calendars, books and magazines both here and abroad, and he writes the route trails for the successful mountain bike magazine, *MTB Pro*. His early education included Outward Bound School where he acquired a love of landscape and gained a deep respect for the countryside, which he has carried with him ever since. He lives in rural Somerset with his partner Kay and they have five children.

WHEELWRIGHT'S
MOUNTAIN BIKE ROUTE GUIDES

THE
COAST-TO-
COAST RIDE

Tim Woodcock

future
BOOKS

Dedication

For Aaron and Kay

First published in 1994 by

Future Books

a division of Future Publishing Limited

Beauford Court, 30 Monmouth Street, Bath BA1 2BW

Text and photographs copyright © Tim Woodcock 1994

Map on pages 6/7 copyright © Estelle Cooke 1994

Route maps based upon the Ordnance Survey mapping with the permission of the

Controller of Her Majesty's Stationery Office © Crown copyright

The moral right of the author has been asserted

Designed by Maria Bowers

A CIP catalogue record for this book is available from the British Library

ISBN: 1 85981 005 5

Printed and Bound by BPC, Paulton Books Ltd.

A member of the British Printing Company

2 4 6 8 10 9 7 5 3 1

If you would like more information on our other cycling titles please write to

The Publisher, Future Books at the above address.

Frontispiece

Late afternoon in Stonesdale

CONTENTS

Barnard Castle

Darlington

Glaisdale

Robin Hoods Bay

Richmond

Grinton

Osmotherley

FINISH

Ripon

The North York Moors

P
e
n
n
i
n
e
s

FOREWORD

The Ride

The Coast-to-Coast is the classic, long distance off-road ride in Britain. It's also the best. Inspired by the idea of Alfred Wainwright's *A Coast-to-Coast Walk* the route passes through our three finest National Parks, crosses England's great watershed and challenges our ingrained preconceptions of the inevitable 'North/South Divide'.

An archetypal view of our island is one of rolling fields, the heavy hand of man shaping the very landscape, but in the old Viking lands of the northern counties landscape has shaped the hand of man. Nowhere on this ride are you far from civilisation, yet the constantly changing scenery is often wild, frequently formidable, and it is apparent that man's efforts at bringing Nature to heel have been diminished. The scars of derelict mine workings, barn dotted dales, a moss-encrusted packhorse bridge, an isolated farm in ruin, an old, grass-covered Roman road; all are absorbed into the land in time, and the prospect is an earth moulded but still untamed.

From the wild and rocky fellsides of the Lakeland Mountains, born of volcanic action millions of years ago, over the bleak, peat moors of the Pennine Ridge, on through the delight of a limestone Dalescape, across the pancake pasture-land of Mowbray and finally to cross the open, heather-clad landscape of the North York Moors there is a great sense of freedom. Freedom born of a landscape that never constrains, of distant horizons and above all by the release that only riding a rough track in wild country can bestow.

The Rider

In the words of the brothers Pepper, native Cumbrian mountain bikers of vast experience, this ride's 'Nay picnic'. And they're right! But then I'm no athlete, am about as skilled on the trail as a hedgehog is on a highway, and forty miles is about as far as I'd ever been in a single ride. Yet every mile was a marvel. I became disdainful of distance and the huge sense of achievement at reaching the North Sea shore was tinged with regret. We almost turned back for a return run west!

But don't get the impression, like so many that follow Wainwright's Way on foot, that it's sufficient to buy the kit and set off. Mountain biking's got about as much in common with fell walking as white-water canoeing has with punting down the Cam. Get some miles, off-road ones, in your legs and then get yourself to St Bees.

The Route

Why start from the Irish Sea shore? The prevailing winds come in from the west and it's no fun fighting them. Go with the flow and ride west to east. The total journey has been split into easy-to-manage legs - roughly 30 miles over eight days - but the fit and experienced off-roader could easily double the distance and halve the time. Alternatively, you could do the ride in sections.

No Cumbria/Yorkshire coast-to-coast route compiler can fail to acknowledge Wainwright as a founding influence, but beyond that this route has little in common with the great man's original. Nor with the current waymarked C-to-C footpath, though the two do coincide from time to time. No, this off-road mountain bike route is as much about the ride as getting from sea-to-sea. In consequence we meander quite a bit in search of the radical, the scenic and quite simply the best off-roading that northern England has to offer. Of course, if it's an A-to-B dash you're after, then by all means plan your own route.

Tim Woodcock,
Somerset, 1994

BEFORE YOU GO

Dozens of folk shock their partners, grab a rucsac, buy a pair of boots and, contrary to all expectations, walk all 180 miles of the waymarked footpath from St Bees to Robin Hood's Bay. Just like that! Fitness, of a pedestrian nature, is found along the way - it takes about three days I'm told - and after that it's amble-time.

Walking is a gentle art. You don't have to be physically fit to tackle long-distance paths, and don't believe those who walk heads down, grass hissing beneath their heels who say you do. Being in shape to bike right across the country is an altogether different thing. You can't pick it up on the trail. And you can't pick it up in the few days before you go. The time to think about getting trim is ten weeks or so before the departure date.

I know it's a long time, puts paid to travelling on a whim and the word 'preparation' rears its ugly head, but being fit will make the whole escapade more fun. For everyone. Even MTBers who get out and hit the hills two or three times a month will benefit from some serious working out on their wheels. By the time you get to St Bees, forty miles, fully laden and off-road, ought not to be an awesome ordeal.

Rides like this are an enriched experience if you're in good company. But travelling companions are notoriously tricky to choose and in the ups and downs betwixt the Irish and North Sea there will be stresses and strains. Long distance off-road is not all fun. On precipitous trails it's both difficult and demanding; add fatigue, perhaps a mis-read map and a ferocious wind and you've got a pretty good recipe for a falling out. Always distressing, discord can soon develop into dispute and that could be dangerous, in the wrong place at the wrong time. Choose companions carefully.

That said, if you take on board the information this book has to offer, you are in for a great ride.

Opposite: Crossing Urra Moor, leaving the storm clouds behind us.

Kitting Out

HARDWARE

'Weight is wearisome'. Whatever you've got, you've got to carry it on this trip. And with about ten passes topping out over the 1500ft contour, you'll appreciate that trimming kit to a necessary minimum makes sense. Providing you don't overdo it, and skimp on essentials, saving weight is safer too. It conserves energy and makes handling the bike on some of the more extreme terrain a lot less hairy. Heavy bikes tend to keep going when they get kicked off course!

The Wheels

We're not going to open and have a good probe about in the can of worms that is 'The Best Bike'. To begin with, bike choice is a personal choice, fads and fashions change on a whim - What of bio-pace? - and providing it's sound, any clunker of an MTB will do. Having said that there are some pointers as to what makes a bike well suited to the task and what does not.

You're going to travel some steep and technical trails so use a good quality, reasonably light, proper MTB - 21 or more indexed gears - with alloy wheels, low gearing and a comfortable saddle. We're talking several hundred pounds here but if you're serious about mountain biking it's worth it. Take a look at the mountain biking press for what's what or ask at a good mountain bike shop. Your bike should also be thoroughly serviced and checked out before setting off. A wheel buckle might well bring an early end to your long awaited trip but a collapse could spell disaster so have your wheels trued before you start.

Some bike accessories that should be considered essential are: bottle cages - back-pack drink carriers and rucsacs don't work well together, top and seat tube padding (closed-cell pipe insulation tube is cheap, waterproof and hard-wearing), a brand new set of the best brake blocks you can afford and some good quality treads with around a two-inch carcass for cushioning and grip. Consult a good MTB bike shop for what's the latest trend in tyres.

Other items to consider, especially if long-distance off-roading really grabs you, are: an aheadset or a headset lock-ring, allen-key crank fittings, a bomb-proof set of wheels, puncture-proof tubes and some sort of suspension, true or otherwise, to fend off fatigue. You may flinch, but fitting pedals and clips and not the ubiquitous SPDs offers a firmer footing when it comes to shouldering that frameset and foot slogging.

Lastly, on this particular trip, there are quite a few road/forest track sections where you might be glad to give the back a rest and dump your kit on a pannier rack. Whatever you do, buy a top quality rack - cheap ones will collapse under the strain - and preferably a hollow-tubed, chromoly one.

Tools and spares

Quality doesn't come cheap but good tools are a godsend when you're in a fix so be prepared to pay for them. Most multi-tools will save weight on a tool-roll of separate bits but don't forget to check that your clever widget does all the whatsits on your bike. And your partners'.

The same goes for spares. If you all run the same tyre valves, chains, straddle wires and even brake blocks, the stores can be kept to a sensible size. Once you've got all tools and spares together pack them tight and keep them handy - ready for the inevitable trail-side emergency. The Coast-to-Coast does take you through England's wildest scenery; even so, there's no need to go over the top with the wilderness thing and go carrying enough spares for a total re-build. Fortunately there are good bike shops that crop up at regular intervals along the way (a list of addresses can be found on pages 92-3).

SOFTWARE

Even in summer, warmth is the vital ingredient, versatility the name of the game. Up on the pass on Walna Scar road it's a lot colder than down by the lake in Coniston. All things being equal, you can be shivering in the icy blast of a savage hailstorm while day-trippers down below are basking in the balmy heat of summer sun, so make sure you are well prepared.

Dress sense

Kitting out a mountain biker has proved to be the outdoor clothes designers' biggest challenge yet. It's a strenuous sport, generates loads of heat at peak activity, then the loonies stand about mending punctures on a hillside with a wind-chill factor of -10°C and their body temperature drops like the proverbial stone. But designers are rising to the challenge and there's a stack of really good, MTB-specific gear to choose from.

The multi-layer principle is one way to go - and it works - but there's always someone who swims against the tide. Companies like Buffalo Clothing, for example, but their pile-lined kit is really late season/winter wear and ideal for weight-saving freaks.

So right from the start we're faced with a bewildering choice of kit, complicated by contrasting design convictions and all so technical that you need a science degree to discern what's what. The best approach is to decide what you want the clothing to do. For long trips it has to be light, have low bulk, be quick-drying, resist the rampant sock syndrome, be easy to care for, fit well, feel comfortable and perform well. Whether it's to wick, provide warmth, windproofing or water resistance, you'll need clothing to perform all of these functions. Above all it has to let your body lose moisture and 'breath'. Under-layer clothing that soaks up water, sags like a wet flannel and dims the lights when the tumble drier's turned on, are useless. Likewise, a top-layer that's built like a tent, flies like a kite and gives you your very own greenhouse effect is best left at home and used as a bin-liner.

Comfort après-trail is fundamental to your well-being. You'll want to ditch the hot dogs, sweaty shirt and humming shorts, have a shower and step into some light longs, slip on a T and put those trail-weary toes into a pair of pliable shoes. Pack-down bulk and weight is especially important with après-trail togs - they'll be on your back most of the time.

On your feet there's nothing to beat a good pair of MTB boots but there are alternatives. Light walking boots and even fell-running shoes, with modified soles, are good alternatives. Both grip well and give ankle support. Don't be tempted by making do with trainers unless you're good at grass skiing with a bike on your back. Some of the carries, especially in the Western Lakes, are

Above: An eventide saunter along Swaledale's ancient cart tracks by Ramps Holme.

arduous, and cleated shoes are bad news too. If you have SPDs think twice about using them - they're not exactly known for being sure-footed on the fellsides.

Last, but definitely not least, wear a helmet!

Navigation aids

Well you can dispense with the bulky package of maps that is the bane of most long-distance rides. They're in the back of the book. Add to that a good quality compass on a neck cord and weather-proof cycle computer - both of which you must be able to use with ease - and that's the pilot part sorted.

Health and Safety

Mountain biking can be dangerous; a minor accident in the mountains of Cumbria or a major fall on the moors of Yorkshire can quickly bring you down to a survival situation. A matter of life or death. Given the right kit, make the right decisions and you can turn crisis into drama, live to tell the tale and even laugh about it. Later. A good first-aid kit and the knowledge of how to use it are essential. A basic kit should include anti-sceptic wipes, plasters, cohesive tape for wounds, triangular bandage, salt tablets for cramp, puritabs and first-aid instructions (first-aid information, covering some of the common MTB emergencies, begins on page 26). You might very well be an accomplished first-aider. Whoever comes to your aid might not and they, not to mention you, will appreciate a set of instructions ready to hand. Survival gear - mini-torch, survival bag and whistle - can all be packed with the first-aid kit.

Pack it in a heavy-duty, zip-tie polythene bag, label it clearly and know where it is.

Not strictly first aid, but pretty important to the health department, are medicaments for treating minor ailments like saddle soreness (not minor if it happens, but Sudacream or E45 cream speeds recovery), athlete's foot, sun burn, lip chaff, muscle strain and pain.

Other stuff

Mountain biking's a dirty business so the personal hygiene department needs careful thought. Apart from the usual salves and unguents for bodily application, some micro wash-liquid is a good idea to keep those shorts clean and fresh on a day-to-day basis. Remember too that you'll need a small, quick-drying towel.

In the bag

Coast-to-Coast walkers will be a common sight on parts of the trail - walk and ride routes coincide from time to time - and many of them stagger along under tower-block backpacks, seams bursting and bedecked in clanking cans. Not so the biker.

A small rucsac - about 30l capacity - together with either a bumbag or a small barbag should be fine. Features to look for are a narrow profile, light weight, waist security strap, wide shoulder straps (easily adjusted and locked), low pack height (try it out, packed full, with your helmet on and look up as though scanning the trail ahead. If the helmet is knocked forwards over your eyes then that's what will happen on the bike; a problem likely to occur with elongated, aero-type helmets), and compression straps. Such features can be found on climbing and fell-running backpacks, but there are a couple of MTB-specific rucsacs that can be swopped from a rider's back to a pannier rack and back again with ease.

If you have problems packing all your kit into thirty-odd litres of space then try rolling the clothes into tight cylinders, holding them down and tying them with compression straps (Velcro straps are ideal). Remember to put the least dense gear at the bottom, the heaviest at the top and ensure the back-panel is comfortable against your spine.

Coast-to-Coast Kit List

A handy, 'pre-flight' check list is provided but don't regard it as definitive - I habitually carry a pair of mini-mulgrips, half a tooth-brush and a pair of earplugs on these trips. I'll leave you to fathom out why. Lists are an important aid to successful trip planning. Try this for starters:

TOOL KIT
Pump
Tyre levers
Full set of Allen keys
Small, adjustable wrench
Screwdriver
(Cross-head and flat)
Chain-splitter
Spoke key
Penknife
BIKE SPARES
Inner tube
Puncture repair kit
Brake blocks
Straddle wire
Rear gear cable
Rear light/batteries
Cable ties
Allen bolts for bottle cages etc
Gaffer/carpet tape
Couple of spare chain links
Cable lock
Water bottle(s)

CYCLE CLOTHING
Padded shorts
(2 pairs min.)
Sports socks
(3 pairs min.)
Cool shirt, short-sleeved
Cycle shirt, long-sleeved
Wicking/thermal top
Bike mitts
Helmet (Not the elongated, aero-type)
Fleece/mid-layer top
Windproof top with hood
Waterproof top
Windproof over-trousers
MTB Boots
APRÈS TRAIL
Light-weight longs
Underwear
Shorts
Baseball boots/sandals or similar

PERSONAL KIT
Wash kit inc. towel
Zipped wallet with money
Plastic
YHA card/B&B contacts
Pencil
Medical kit
Head torch/batteries
TRAIL KIT
Compass
Computer
First-aid Kit
Survival kit
(Whistle, bag, torch)
Emergency food
(Cereal bars etc.)
Rucsac with liner
Bar/bum bag (to keep emergency kit separated)

If you're expecting cold, wet weather then you'll need to add extra clothing, especially thermals (tights, tops and socks), full gloves, headband/snood and waterproof socks. In winter an extra-warm fleece/windproof top, lined mitts and lined hood may be necessary for when you're caught in the open with an emergency repair. Finally, don't forget lights - you may be caught out in the dark.

How heavy will all this weigh? For a summer crossing aim for about 14lbs for your personal kit and about 7lbs of shared gear (including food). With three up that's about 16lbs of kit each.

Accommodation

From the outset one of the key considerations is where you are going to sleep. Even how you are going to sleep. Comfort and a good night's rest are keynotes to the success of long-distance cycling, and only you will know what your absolute needs are. Consider them carefully - you owe it to yourself.

Camping
Camping and self-sufficiency seem to go hand-in-hand with the adventure of mountain biking but - and it's a big but - the penalties are high. Tent, stove, sleeping bag, mat, cooking kit and food plus additional clothes and the out-sized rucsac to put it all in will weigh you down by an extra stone or so and make pass-storming sheer purgatory. Descents are interesting though, if lethal! Survivors, exhausted by a day beneath their burden, will then have the pleasure of finding a pitch, setting the tent, searching out a stream, fetching the water and washing cold. Then it's cook, eat, clean-up and finally fall into a stupor only to be driven spare at the crack of dawn by a demented bunch of birds doing their dawn chorus thing! Camping's great.

Bed and Breakfast
By way of comparison, at the opposite extreme, we have B&Bs. First and foremost you can dump all that camping kit and ride light. Not day-ride light, but nimble enough to loft wheels, bunny hop and skip the rear end round the odd rock. And that's handy. It's fun too! Add to that an end-of-day cuppa followed by

a hot bath, supper in the pub, uninterrupted sleep and a breakfast to build a day's trail blazing on and you've got luxury. But it costs and, in season, pre-booking is advisable. That means a timetable.

Youth Hostels

Somewhere between the two alternatives are Youth Hostels. You need only carry the same kit as for B&Bs, and they're much cheaper. Most provide a full range of services from shop to showers and if you're not the self-catering-type, breakfast and evening meal can be a convenient opt-out. Add to that the best YHA idea - the drying room - and you can see hostels are handy. On the downside mucking in with a bunch of strangers night-on-night isn't always ideal, accommodation is single-sex and in dormitories. But, all in all, hostels are the best bet and on this route coast-to-coasters are well catered for.

Passing through three National Parks the route has a liberal sprinkling of YHAs along its length - although there's a big gap in the middle of the North York Moors - and these are listed separately (see p. 92). Pre-booking is prudent in high-season and many hostels, like B&Bs, have a closed season so the logistics of a winter crossing need more careful planning.

Below: Towards the end of the day, the prospect of a hot shower and good grub seems very inviting.

ON THE RIDE

Getting There

Most likely the Coast-to-Coast will be a one-way journey and that probably means getting to the Cumbrian coast by train.

British Rail is not known for being biker-friendly so the key rule is to check, re-check and book everything in advance. Bikes especially! Carlisle (0228 44711) is the mainline gateway to the Lake District and the rolling stock used will take three or four bikes. Not all the trains go to St Bees but they do all go to Whitehaven just five miles north of the start point.

Of course you can leave the car at the start and ride a round trip, persuade a long-suffering friend or partner to come and pick you up or even have the fortune to organise a taxi service. There are three main road routes west from the M6. In the south it's the A590 to the A595 off junction 36, distance 65 miles; from the east it's the A66 to the A595 off junction 40 at Penrith, distance 50 miles; from the north it's the A7 to the A595 off junction 44 north of Carlisle, distance 45 miles.

If you are only doing part of the route, then the day-by-day route instructions give the nearest railway station to the start and end of each day's ride. Check out the times of trains and whether they will carry your bike before you set out.

Getting home

Robin Hood's bay isn't on a railway line. Well, it is, but it's dismantled. So it's nice to cock-a-snoop at British Rail, who off-loaded this branch line for an absolute pittance, and use the route anyway. As a cycle path. Both Scarborough, a fifteen-mile ride south, and Whitby, a six-mile cruise north, have railway stations and passenger information is available from Darlington (091 232 6262). Although you can turn up on the off-chance that you, your friends and all your bikes will be able to catch a train it's smart to book. The bike-carrying capacity of the rolling stock run on these routes varies from one to four(ish).

The A171 is the main route through the east side of the North York Moors and passes just a couple of miles west of the Bay. Once again Whitby (with Middlesborough and Darlington beyond) to the north and Scarborough to the south are the gateways.

Fell-Riding

Ride safe. Ride light. Being the new boys on the block, mountain bikers have run the gauntlet of being alienated by other countryside users since the word go. The sport has mushroomed and our wilderness areas have witnessed a wheeled invasion - ramblers see us as rivals, environmentalists call us erosionists and farmers fear speeding bikes will frighten stock and uncaring cyclists will flatten crops.

The fact that it's a re-run of early rambler versus landowner conflicts makes no difference. But we're here to stay and attitudes will inevitably change and change quickly if we ride responsibly.

Rights of Way

Although we've taken every care to try and ensure that the Coast-to-Coast route will keep your cycling within the law, at the very least the status of some sections is likely to change. Plus, of course, you may get lost so it is as well to be sure of your rights of way.

Off-road cycling is permitted on bridleways, roads used as public paths (RUPPs), by-ways open to all traffic (BOATs), unclassified county roads and designated cycle paths. Some of the Forestry Commission and North-West Water Authority roads are open to us with the landowner's consent and this permissive access may be revoked at any time. Cycling is not permitted on footpaths, open land or on pavements. Do not rely on signposts as reliable indicators of a route's status - local authorities do not always make correct use of bridleway (Blue) and footpath (Yellow) waymarkers. If in doubt dismount. And remember, all land is owned by someone - even in the three National Parks on this route - and you must take care not to trespass. If a landowner asks you to leave it is in your best interests, no matter what the right and wrong of it may be, to acquiesce.

Of course you may be bowling along a bridleway when up pops a barbed wire fence and the way is barred. It's a tricky situation because your rights are wrapped in a woolly bit of rhetoric which says you can remove the obstacle sufficiently to get past if it is reasonably possible, or make a short detour to get round it. The landowner can demand recompense if you cause any damage so clambering over it - often the instinctive reaction - is not a clever thing to do. This doesn't happen often but Rights of Way across farmland do get blocked, ploughed up, are over-planted or are stocked with dangerous animals. Farmers are supposed to provide signed, alternative routes but if you're in doubt don't traipse across regardless. Check with the owner and if you're still forced off the Right of Way report it to the local authority - addresses are given on page 93 - who will take up the matter on your behalf.

Codes of conduct

In following the Coast-to-Coast off-road route you will be treading in the tyre tracks of others. If they've careered along, forged furrows across fields, stampeded livestock, left gates gaping and created a trail of havoc and mayhem, then you're not going to get a warm reception from the locals. Nor is anybody else who follows behind. So, follow the Country and Off-road Codes.

 # THE COUNTRY CODE

- Enjoy the countryside and respect its life and work
- Guard against all risk of fire
- Fasten all gates
- Keep dogs under control
- Keep to Public Rights of Way across farmland
- Use gates and stiles to cross boundaries
- Leave livestock, crops and machinery alone
- Take your litter home
- Do not contaminate water
- Protect wild flora and fauna
- Take special care on country roads
- Make no unnecessary noise
- Cycle only on permitted Rights of Way
- Give way to horse riders and walkers
- Do not ride in such a manner that you are a danger to others
- Do not race
- Keep erosion to a minimum and do not skid
- Be courteous and considerate to others
- Be self-sufficient and make sure your bike is safe to ride
- Wear a helmet
- Follow a route marked on a map
- Follow the Country Code

They're not really a set of rules so much as guidance that any responsible, thoughtful member of the mountain biking community would adopt without a second's thought.

Ride safety

Three's company, not two, and four's fine outdoors in the wilds. In the event of one getting badly injured someone can go for help and someone can stay with the casualty. But ideally two should go for help, not one, which is why four is better. Any more, and mountain bikers in a bunch can be an intimidating party on a narrow path.

Abilities, strength and stamina in any group will vary. Keep within the capacity of everyone, watch your pace and make sure everyone keeps within sight and sound of each other. But don't bunch up, especially on downhills, or there'll be some rear-end wipe-outs. And they can be real nasty! It's always a good idea to wait for stragglers at the top of climbs, at the bottom of tricky descents and at gates. It's in the nature of a strung out group to separate even further at such points, so make sure that the young, eager pup out in front is aware of it.

One of the first signs of fatigue is when your normally ebullient companion rides quiet and persistently lags behind. Don't push it, it's not worth it. Rest, drink, eat and keep warm - exposure may

Below: After some radical rock hopping on Walna Scar Road you can gain your composure where it turns to hardpack.

be just around the corner. Prevention is better than cure. Eat heartily at supper and breakfast. Don't be over-confident when assessing how much of the Coast-to-Coast you can do in one day. Don't ride for more than an hour without eating some food, and drink regularly, before you get thirsty. Always wear enough to keep warm and if you stop in cold weather, put an extra layer on.

Weather

Out in the wilds, weather will make or break a day. In northern England it's notoriously variable and up in the fells it's all in a day's ride to experience sun, sleet, rain, wind, warmth, cold and calm. Maybe our mountains are small on the global scale but they don't act like it. It's easy to be lulled into a false sense of security, set out ill-informed and unprepared and end up the subject of a fell rescue operation. Get the most recent weather forecast - telephone numbers are given on page 92 - and catch the latest TV weather forecasts. They give a useful overview of what's coming.

   Three factors that strangers to the fells often fail to take into account are altitude, wind and winter. As you climb temperature falls. Roughly speaking temperature falls $1C°$ for every 100m gain in height ($3C°$ per 1000ft) on a clear day, half that fall on a cloudy one. Wind-chill, the cooling effect of cold air passing over warm bodies, increases with wind strength. In a gentle to moderate breeze (Force 3, about 10mph) wind-chill is about $-5C°$, about $-10C°$ in a fresh, gusty breeze (Force 5, about 20mph) and $-15C°$ in a really strong wind (Force 7, about 30mph).

   It would be foolish to venture out into the Cumbrian Mountains if strong winds are forecast - they'll be more ferocious on the higher fells. For example, on a clear, calm day the temperature on Black Sail Pass will be about $5C°$ colder than down in the garden of Ennerdale YHA. Add in the cooling effect of the inevitable wind, say a brisk breeeze, and up on the Pass temperatures will dip a chilling $12C°$ or so! Even in summer temperature frequently falls to $5°C$, in mid-winter we're talking down another $10\text{-}14C°$. That's $9°$ below zero! Makes you think, doesn't it?

   Forecasts give temperatures but it's as well to bear in mind, when planning a departure date, that winter temperatures will be $10\text{-}15C°$ colder than summer ones. Nippy!

Losing your way

Navigation can be tricky. Keeping on course depends on you, and your companions, knowing your position at ALL times. Danger zones are forests, open moor and in poor visibility, so take care to read the terrain correctly in these situations and make no assumptions about this or that trail being a 'main' route. One way of coping with poor visibility is to follow a compass bearing to the most distant visible marker (not a sheep because it might walk off!), cycle to it, take another bearing on the next marker, cycle and so on. With very few exceptions - over to Mosedale and Wet Sleddale is one - you'll be riding on obvious tracks and paths so you are more likely to feel lost than really be lost.

But, despite our best endeavours to keep you on track, there's always a chance you might wander from the route. Nobody intends to get lost and it comes as a shock. Don't panic. Stop. Make sure everybody's with you and then try to work out where you went wrong. Not too far back you'll have been sure of your position. Find it on the map. If you have been using your cycle computer to keep a log of point-to-point distances, it is then a simple matter of reading the distance off, calculating direction and that'll give you an approximate position. Forgotten to zero the trip distance at the last known point? Then estimate how long ago you were there and in which direction you have travelled during the elapsed time. Allowing for ground conditions, calculate how far you've cycled. Now check your surroundings and see if local landmarks coincide with your findings. If you're still unsure and visibility is poor then stay put until conditions improve.

In an ideal world three distinct landmarks should be recognised for you to be absolutely certain of your locality though, given two, you can still take compass bearings to position yourself. Correct use of the compass and trusting it, not your instincts, is vital.

Accident Procedure

It's vital too that at least one of the party is a qualified first-aider. Ideally all of you should know the fundamentals of first aid. The British Red Cross, St John's Ambulance and St Andrew's Ambulance Societies all run courses so, if you haven't done already, book into one. One day, somebody will thank you for it.

It cannot be over-emphasised that carrying a proper first-aid kit with instructions and being a competent first aider is an essential part of accident procedure. Listed below are the most common illnesses and injuries relating to mountain biking:

Hypothermia

(Exposure - the most common cause for rescue calls)

SYMPTONS:

Complaints of fatique; cold, visual abnormalities; Lethargy, lack of interest; Cold, clammy skin, pale in colour; Slurred speech; Cramps; Clumsiness; Odd behaviour; out of character actions; Collapse and coma.

ACTION:

Stop. Do not continue in the hope that you'll find shelter.

Shelter the patient. Wrap them in extra clothing and put them in the survival bag, with someone else if possible. If you have a sleeping bag then use it as an inner layer.

Warm the patient with bodily companionship and a warm drink if possible. Easily digested energy food can be given provided the patient is not too drowsy.

Cheer the patient up - low moral is a contributory factor. Be positive - the rest of the group will be feeling pretty worried.

Rest the patient for a prolonged period. If there's any doubt about the patient's ability to recover then send for help.

Look for signs of exposure in other members of the party and signs of frostbite if conditions are severe.

Do not rub the patient to restore circulation

Do not give alcohol - it may cause collapse.

In extreme cases, patients sometimes stop breathing so be prepared to give mouth-to-mouth, and if the patient does lose consciousness place them in the recovery position.

Seek Medical Help

Frostbite

(Long descents and winds in winter are common causes)

SYMPTOMS:

Prickling pain; Numbness; Skin may discolour blue or white; Skin may feel hard

ACTION:

Warm the affected area with additional body heat only.

Extremities are the most commonly affected areas and can be placed in the armpit or crotch. The face can be smothered with dry, gloved hands.

Remove rings, watches, boots etc to ensure free blood flow.

Do not rub the affected area.

Do not apply heat from an artificial source.

Do not use a re-vitalized limb or the affected tissue will tear.

Seek Medical Help

Heat Exhaustion

(Common during periods of sustained effort)

SYMPTOMS:

Pale, sweaty skin; Complaints of dizziness, fatigue and headache; Cramps; Rapid but weak pulse; shallow breathing; Fainting

ACTION:

Shade the patient. Find a cool,

shady spot and lie them down.
Cold drinks of water, slightly salted and with a little sugar if possible, will soon aid recovery.
Seek Medical Help.

Heatstroke
(Severe heat exhaustion)
SYMPTOMS:
Restlessness; Frequent passing of urine; Complaints of dizziness and headache; Hot, flushed, dry skin; Rapid, strong pulse; Fainting
ACTION:
Cool the patient by placing them in shade and remove their clothing.
Sponge their body with water until their body temperature drops and they appear to recover.
Seek Medical Help Immediately

Shock
(Present in almost all cases of traumatic accidents)
SYMPTOMS:
Pale and pallid skin, especially the lips; Rapid, weak pulse; Rapid, shallow breathing; Cold, sweaty skin; Complaints of dizziness and blurred vision; Restlessness; Yawning, pronounced sighing; Fainting
ACTION:
Reassure the patient.
External bleeding or other injuries should be treated simultaneously.
Lie the patient down, but keep warm and avoid unnecessary movement.
Turn their head to one side.
Raise their feet on a pile of clothes or small rucsac.
Loosen restrictive clothing.
Control Body Temperature with loose clothing.
Do not give food or drink.

Do not apply heat from an artificial source.
Seek Medical Help Immediately

Dislocation
(Elbow, shoulder and knee joints are most at risk)
SYMPTOMS:
Deformity of the joint, especially when compared to the joint on the opposite side of the body; Swelling around the joint; Lack of mobility; Severe pain associated with the joint
ACTION:
Support the injured limb in a comfortable position.
Do not try to manipulate the joint.
Do not move the affected joint unnecessarily. **Seek Medical Help**

Broken Collar Bone
(Perhaps the most common MTB fracture)
SYMPTOMS:
Patient supports injured arm against the body; Head inclined towards the injured shoulder; Lack of mobility in the injured side; Swelling at the front of injured shoulder
ACTION:
Position arm of injured side with fingers up towards the opposite shoulder, palm flat against the body, so far as the patient will allow. Place soft padding between the upper arm and body. Support the arm using the triangular bandage for an elevation sling off the good shoulder that encloses the elbow, forearm and hand.
Secure the arm against the body with a belt or strap that encircles the body.
Do not move the injured arm if it is too painful, support against the body in situ. **Seek Medical Help**

THE COAST-TO-COAST RIDE

Setting Out

Eyed by an intrigued local we posed for the album snap. Backs to an ice-blue Irish Sea, choppy waves whipped up by a cutting nor-westerly, we were keen to kick the cranks and get going. Facing us was 210 miles of road, trail and single-track that started right there, under our wheels, and would end where Yorkshire slides beneath the North Sea at Robin Hood's Bay. The prospect was worth savouring. But not for long.

A last look - or so we thought - at the mountainous mass of the Isle of Man set amid the glittering sea and we set off in high spirits, helped by that gutsy west wind. It would prove to be both friend and foe in the following days. Soon the Cumbrian mountains jutted above the eastern horizon - the sight spurred us to spin over the hill for Mirehouse.

Down amongst the ranks of new estate houses we got lost looking for the Rowrah cycle-path. But a young lass pedalling a shopper three-speed came to our rescue and kindly lead us to it. The tarmac ribbon makes for a surrealist ride. Its slick, black surface hummed busily under the heavy treads as we weaved our way between local traffic, heads down and with our mind on the mountains. Into Rowrah's old station car park and the tyres got a christening on the short unmetaled run to the lane near Lamplugh school. The climb to Kelton Fell gave us a twisty dip to Croasdale which, in our zest for speed, gave us some heart-stopping tyre skips as we courted disaster on the chicanes. Not good!

Evening sun sliced through a cleft in the dark cloud mass, flooding Ennerdale with a chiaroscuro of golds and greens above the deep slate-blue of Ennerdale Water. A sudden realisation. Here we were, cruising up a mountain valley on a dirt road. Our coast-to-coast was truly under way! All too soon we came upon the familiar YHA sign and, with the smell of wood smoke hanging in the air, we signed in.

Black Sail Pass to Boot

We'd planned crack of dawn departures but - and this set a precedent - we finally got the cranks turning at ten. Ennerdale Forest was shrouded in damp, pine-scented mists and soon we were humming past coast-to-coast hikers who had the drop on us when it came to early starts. It was a sobering sight to see the massive packs they were struggling under.

Out of the trees, and smooth forest fire-road gave onto rock-strewn bridleway. This was more like it! Approaching the isolated cottage of Black Sail we got our first glimpse of the 1800ft Black Sail Pass. Tiny figures of hikers laboriously scaled the distant fellside. A daunting prospect, Black Sail looked insurmountable! Then the cloud base dropped like a silent curtain and it was gone. On the far side the Wasdale descent had been billed by some as the best in the Lakes. A strong incentive to crest the col and relish the moment our wheels dropped towards Wasdale. First came the carry - 860ft of it. Rackpacks quickly converted to backpacks and, with framesets shouldered, we scrambled up the precipitous fellside.

We surprised ourselves with an impressive amount of height-gain in return for modest efforts. As we crested the col the cloud base lifted and we were treated to a fine view of lofty peaks'n' passes. From the col's lip we viewed the drop to Wasdale with dismay. Virtually sheer, the scree-strewn path presented an unridable prospect for the first few hundred yards and even then it was a hair-raising run to Gatherstone Ford. There was no stopping us until we ploughed into some rutted zig-zags - those packs add more speed than full suspension! Beyond the ford the gradient eased for a faster run-out to Wasdale Head.

Always a bit of a honey-pot, the hamlet was crawling with continental student trekkers. We breezed on through. The sun made a late entrance, sparkled bright on spray droplets as we

Overleaf (main picture): Eyes down and ignore the view. Aaron negotiates the famous Z's down into Wasdale. Inset: Storming Black Sail Pass - an impressive 860ft scramble from the valley below.

splashed through Wasdale's fords skirting the lower slopes of Scafell's massive form. The climb-out onto Burnmoor proved too rubbly to ride - my companion, Aaron, tried again and again to get the cranks turning, but gave up in disgust - so the turf-sprung descent to Burnmoor Tarn came as a delight.

Skirting the Tarn's water-logged northern shore we pressed on to Eller How, eager for the long descent into Boot, and grateful for the regular cairns that marked the way. As the track dropped away Aaron let out a whoop of delight. The day's hard climbing was bagged and gravity was going our way again! He pumped the pedals until every bit of rock kicked him airborne. Suddenly his steel steed pranced sideways, the backpack's weight amplifying imbalance to the point of disaster. In a split microsecond, on pure instinct, he hauled his wayward wheels back into line and careered off onto turf. Breath regained, and control restored, he dropped in behind me and we cruised into Boot at a more considered speed, scattering the suicidal chickens by the mill. After a late afternoon ice-cream we ambled down the short stretch of road to the YHA pleased to end the day on such a superb descent.

Over Walna to Windermere

The morning kicked off with a mile of tarmac. Barely sufficient to turn stiff leg muscles into the supple dynamos we'd hoped they'd be. Could they really last? We had to conquer the 2000ft pass of Brown Pike on the Walna Scar road later in the day. We dipped down onto the bridleway that skirts Birker Fell. An aromatic mix of damp bracken and pine scents filled the air and filled our lungs as we toiled up the steep slope below Dod Knott.

Aaron, keen to put more miles between us and the West coast, just about made the summit with a heroic honk'n'feather routine. But his ego flattened faster than snake bitten butyl at the sight of the Irish Sea - ten miles down the dale! If only he'd been looking the other way - the Scafells made a magnificent mountain panorama.

The smell of rain was in the westerly wind, and with that we pressed on over a boggy col and into Dunnerdale Forest's dark, damp interior. Riding was well nigh impossible. Slimy roots swiped front-tyres, smooth boulders bounced us into bogs and the bogs buried wheels beyond hub depth. That half-mile seemed endless but at last we made the forest road. A lumberjack directed us off the bridleway - it looked like more of the same - and onto a fire-road to Grassguards ford. We blasted down that track on a heady mix of high speed and hardpack, the slip-stream whistling in our ears.

Down by the ford we took on some more technical single-track. It dipped and dived, threw in some slick-rock and rubble before a near sheer slide down to the River Duddon. Brilliant! We almost fetched up in the water. Aaron, with a bike on his back, did a 'Torvil and Dean' impression on the stepping stones, scored 9 points for artistic interpretation, zero for technical merit and I had to help him out - after I'd stopped laughing. But merriment soon ceased when midges attacked en-masse and we high-tailed it for the road.

Rain was now upon us. Above, hidden in massed ranks of drizzle, loomed the sodden ridge of Walna Scar. Turf and rock glistened in the downpour, traction disappeared, and it was down to a push'n'pedal slog up Walna Scar Side. We kept telling ourselves that we'd ride it all if it weren't for the rucsacs and rain. Maybe. Aaron had faltered to a shadow of his previous performance up Birker Fell, so we took ten and watched the cloud base descend. The track turns across the slope here and, to prove we weren't destined to walk to Robin Hood's Bay, we mounted up, stressed those reluctant calf muscles and honked it over the pass.

Nothing like killing a hill to revive ragged spirits. We hammered on down a tasty bit of trail, skirting the slopes of the venerable Old Man of Coniston, his head in the clouds. Abruptly it all turned steep, serpentine and mega-rocky. A track to test our technical skills to the limit and beyond. We tasted turf but got away with it. I hummed a ditty in praise of shock forks. Lower down boulder-strewn track gave way to a more civilised trail and our jellied legs were given a chance to turn the cranks. All of a sudden we burst out of the clouds and into sun! Coniston and

Overleaf (left): Turf rounds off the rough'n'ready road into Boot. Watch out for the chickens at the Mill. Right: The Duddon step-stones where a sure foot, or two, and three hands would be a distinct advantage.

Grizedale lay, Lilliputian in scale, below and on came the heat - we'd forgotten it was mid-summer! With the hammer down we hit the tarmac flying, our speed destined to dish out thrills and near spills on the S-bends above Coniston.

We simmered in warm sun, lunched and played tourist in Coniston. The bikes had taken a real pummelling and a quick rim check revealed that a rear wheel needed some torsional attention. It was well into the afternoon so we had to make those pedals hum if we were to get to Ambleside in time to have it trued.

Up to High Tiberthwaite - where we witnessed a farmer hand-shearing his sheep - and into the rugged Langdale region. A complex mix of folded slate, fell and field with crags and crannies, the landscape here is criss-crossed by a myriad of mining tracks and is a delight to ride. We pumped up the speed and, with time out to savour the scenery along Loughrigg Terrace and saunter along Rydal Water's shore, we cruised into Ambleside, mud-splattered and glad to have made it in time for the shops. It's a real tourist hot-spot. Choc-a-block with a bustling, bright pot-pourri of visitors from all over the world, Ambleside certainly gave us a quick slap of culture-shock.

Once we had the wheel sorted, demolished an ice-cream or two we got stuck into the climb-out to Jenkin's Crag. A granny-cog slog but the rewards are worth it. Stupendous views over Windermere. In the evening light it was a scene of sylvan beauty but it was still a fair few miles to High Cross YHA. Reluctantly we moved off. Late evening saw us turn into the YHA's drive. Were we glad to hit the sack that night!

Dash for the Dales

Serried ranks of rain slashed the hostel windows, driven by a baleful wind. Breakfast was eaten in sombre mood. My hopes for fine weather on this of all days - the longest leg over muddy moors traversed by faint trails - looked forlorn. A quick call to the Lakes weatherline left me with a surfeit of doom-laden met-speak ringing in my ears: 'deepening depression', 'atrocious conditions', 'winds gusting storm force' and 'visibility down to 100m'. Where's my hip flask!

For once we set off with calf muscles in fine fettle, we'd settled down to packs on backs and our appetite for storming the passes ahead had been whetted by trekkers' tales of rock-strewn tracks, twisty and steep. Garburn Road was a real desolate spot, enshrouded in mist, puddled and marked by the corpse of a sheep. Despite Nature's efforts to dampen our mood we felt pretty good. We'd conquered the first climb, were well ahead of schedule and some hot downhilling was imminent.

A terse note on the map 'rocky/steep/tricky' proved that forewarned is not necessarily forearmed. When Kentmere came into sight, speed overtook caution, I overtook the bike and the last thing I remember seeing was a rock with my name on it. Closing fast. Bang! Split brow. Lot's of blood, I felt dented and dazed and it looked like the end of the trip. But Aaron - his nausea of gore firmly controlled - did a great patch-up job and saved both the day and the trip.

Distinctly groggy I walked down to the hamlet where we searched in vain - and in the rain - for a hot cuppa. It's afternoon teas only in Kentmere so we pressed on. With 30 miles still to go we now had a good idea of how Noah felt. Wet!

Thankfully the climb past Stile End proved kid's stuff by comparison to what we'd scaled to date but the drop to Sadgill - marked by another 'steep/rocky' note on the map - was a real test of trail skills. Especially a treacherous zig-zag that had us slip-sliding down the fellside into Sadgill. Crossing the bridge exposed us to the gale's full fury. It tore up Longsleddale and we were blasted up the valley until we hit a bizarre bit of paving. The slippery slope, more like an inclined ice-rink, proved unrideable. We walked, found shelter behind a rough stone wall and watched the rain rush past; now a 3:1 mix with hail. Visibility was as per the met forecast and the howling wind had reduced communication to a mono-syllabic shouting match. Of the Mosedale bridleway there was no sign, just a wet, wooden finger pointing into the swirling mist. Compass time.

After half an hour's bog trotting, the gate on Brownhowe hove into view and I knew then that we were on track. Mind you the sodden trail into Mosedale was barely discernible. Nor was the

Overleaf: One of Wordsworth's favourite haunts, Rydal Water offers fat-tyre freaks a chance to wet their threads.

dark shape of the Cottage when it first appeared through the torrential rain. Now I knew the worst was over. Aaron described it as the most heart-lifting sight he'd ever seen and this shelter from the storm certainly seemed heaven-sent. Once inside the silence was awesome. We stood, arms akimbo, and water dripping from our sleeves. Time for dry kit, food and restoration. We donned pertex trousers, replaced our sodden tops and emerged from the cottage ready for the fray.

The storm lashed the tattered roof of the cottage, the rain ran horizontal and the wind howled. Time for a route change. Wet Sleddale might sound appropriate but we opted for the shorter and, we had been told, more defined detour into Swindale. The definition of 'defined' needs defining; the bridleway to Swindale was definitely very faint. In fact invisible to my eye (the other one had closed up by now). Map and compass mode again.

Following the map-marked way we contoured the spur and our path came and went in fits and starts before finally asserting its right of passage. So involved was I in trying to make do with single vision that the precipitous drop into Swindale almost caught me out. Aaron was already on his way. I followed, bum over the back wheel to gain traction. Zippo! Wet grass. We might as well have had slicks, and my blocks just let the rims slide by. Talk about being committed - it was a downhill ski run, not a ride!

Under the lee of Selside Crags we paused for breath and watched water cascade off the cliffs. That was a real tempest up there. Down onto Swindale's lane, rolling resistance disappeared and that howling westerly turbo-charged us down the vale and we were sheltering in Shap chippy in next to no time. Lighter by four gallons of water - this was masquerading as a lake on the cafe floor - and buoyed up by chips and coffee the last leg to Kirkby was a real breeze. Literally! We signed in at the YHA nine hours after leaving High Cross - despite mishaps and chip stops - exhausted, but well pleased.

Halfway Inn

By the time we'd finished a much needed bit of bike 'R&R', Kirkby Stephen was well into its lunchtime bustle. The day was bright, breezy and the air had a springtime nip. It certainly put a spring in the step of a herd of heifers down in the Belah valley - they chased us all the way up on to the moor. Safely beyond the bridle-gate we searched in vain for the map-marked bridleway. In the end we followed hoof marks and footprints on a path up by the forest and onto the road.

Crossing England's watershed was next on the venue. We were full of curiosity to see how such an important demarcation would look. After all, a drop of rain, plummeting towards the Pennine ridge could wind up in the North or Irish Sea; its destiny decided on a breath of wind and a whim of Nature. So we set off along the ridge road to find that, east or west, the water's course is actually determined on a bleak col marked by a non-descript, grey building. For me the Tan Hill Inn is the real watershed - a proper watering hole too.

On joining the Pennine Way we expected to encounter walkers - the peaty trail looked well-used - but the bleak weather must have put them off. We pressed on towards Swaledale where I'd scheduled a summer eventide's cruise down to Grinton and, amazingly, the wind dropped and Nature delivered golden sun right on cue. We lingered on a hill above Stonesdale, captivated by the beauty of the pastoral scene below. Only the promise of some brilliant hammertime galvanised us into action. We'd imagined that Swaledale would be all riverside farm tracks and a laid-back saunter through hay fields. But in our initial peruse of the map we'd missed the tight contours that betrayed a steep descent from Crackpot into Swinnergill.

It lived right up to expectations. Hugging the side of a gorge gouged out by the infant Swale, the gritty track drops down the flank of Stony Hill - the name gives away the game - for a top-cogging skip'n'run before diving down a hair-raising chicane into Swinnergill itself.

There's just enough rut and rubble to make hammering a touch risky and, if someone opens the gate, there's a final chill-out in the ford to kill the mph. Brilliant! The epitome of a great off-road

Overleaf (left): The author scales Belah valley with a herd of heifers in hot pursuit - just beyond the wall. Right: Swaledale - a pastoral scene that must have gladdened the hearts of fellow travellers for more than fifty generations.

descent. But evening was drawing in and we still had 10 miles to go! Lengthening shadows overtook us as we made our way down ancient, over-grown farm tracks alongside the river Swale. The smell of freshly-mown hay and bird-song filled the air and we ambled along, finally making the short pull up to Grinton YHA as the sun set.

Motoring to the Moors

The early morning sun grazed the dew-laden meadows of Swaledale below Grinton Lodge's courtyard. A nip to the air but the sun was a welcome change. Scattered over the flagstones were casualties of the pedestrian coast-to-coast tending to tenderised toes, burst blisters and other aches and pains peculiar to pilgrims of Wainwright's Way. Bikers evidently fare better; prangs apart we had no sprains and strains to complain of.

Where were we? Morning five. By now days were fusing together distinguished only by events, ascents and descents. Today, like yesterday, should be a cruise: off-road to Richmond then the pancake run to Osmotherley YHA over on the western fringe of the North York Moors. Reeth looked serene in the morning sun - Constable would have loved it - but despite the rural pastiche our rustic trail still packed in a couple of stiff climbs and hammertime downhills before we hit town. And, while I remember, some bike-hostile stiles at Applegarth that frayed tempers. To make matters worse, we did see a parallel track to use; after the last stile.

Richmond is full of teashops so we treated ourselves to munchies and ignored the arched eyebrows of the polite clientele. Mud-splattered legs and lycra shorts may be frowned upon but we still crooked our little fingers, drank our tea and paid up nicely. Richmond also boasts a formidable fortress - the founding of the town - and a stroll round the battlements was the perfect post-lunch constitutional.

The ever-present westerlies were allies today, increasing our average speed, and we blasted across the Vale of Mowbray at 25mph. The views were spectacular and the riding a dream. Our passage was punctuated by a string of plodding coast-to-coast hikers, toting high-rise packs and resembling astronauts on a moon-walk. We breezed on by, under the A1, straight through Osmotherley and into the YHA bang on opening time.

Pale Trails to Glaisdale

We woke hungry for the trails. By breakfast time we'd packed and it was a case of eat up and go. During the morning repast some unkind hiker mentioned the naughty 'P' word ('puncture' for the uninitiated) and asked, by way of making conversation, how many had we sustained so far? We winced and from then on the Finger of Fate was pointed right at my rear wheel.

Out on Scarth Wood Moor we hit prime-time trail blasting on some demon-speed descents with a dusting of technicalities to skip over. Here our route coincided with the Cleveland Way but, as luck was with us, walkers were few and far between. Brilliant for clear runs but all good things come to an end. Down in Scugdale we forsook gritty track for tarmac to climb the valley, past Scugdale Hall - where the sign dwarfs the house. A short stretch of track before the final haul up onto Stoney Wicks gave us a quick taste of tricky single-track. There we encountered a pair of wild cyclo-crossers; skinny treads and all! Strange breed. Why run about the moors with a road bike on your back when fat tyres give you the freedom to ride?

On the Wicks a heather-clad moorland panorama provided our first real views of the National Park, before we dropped down to Raisdale on a bizarre piece of bridleway that clung tenaciously to the top of a V-shaped ravine. A bit of fine balancing and we both made it to the mill below for a quick romp on the road to Seave Green. Lunchtime was reminiscent of a real picnic for once - we actually had sun to bathe in - but before we could break out the suntan lotion, down came the rain. Back to Windshirt weather again! Climbing up East Bank through the still air of a steaming pine plantation, beset by buzzing flies and with just about zero grip, tested power'n'feather technique to the limit. And patience.

Beyond the trees a sedge-covered gully cut a boggy path up onto a dyke. Finally we made the top where a fresh breeze whisked

Overleaf (left): The Swale viewed from Richmond Castle, a fortress built to guard the river crossing. Right: Dirt track with a touch of technical, that's Scarth Wood Moor's opener for the North York Moors.

away the irritating insects and cooled our fevered brows. Way out on the western horizon the Pennine ridge stood grey and remote. We'd cycled from there and, before that, from as far as the eye could see. It felt good. Not so good were the menacing clouds, distinctly thunderous and heading our way. Heat shimmered off the dark heather and we burned along cream-coloured tracks in an effort to out-run the rain. But it wasn't rain we tried in vain to avoid, it was hail. Along the exposed edge of Greenhow Bank we caught it broadside. In an instant the hail hammered our knees pink and the wind buffeted us about like a pair of drunken pedlars. Unbelievable! Thankfully the storm was short-lived, if vicious, and the sun re-appeared as we crested the summit of Burton Howe. We took ten, munched cereal bars and took in the distant views. The air was crystal-clear.

Coming down off the Howe the loose rock of a recently reinstated shooting track kept us on a technical edge and threw in a couple of stylish endos. Thankfully the heather provided a soft(ish) embrace. Up on Baysdale Moor we delighted in burning along at warp speed, hopping tricky bits and skipping side-to-side on the best lines. My treat was that inevitable flat and it had to be a snake bite.

Towards Westerdale we ran into a zany piece of single-track. Random boulders created a crude slalom trail. Fine in the dry but treacherous in the wet. Under wheels those round-shouldered rocks called for real dexterity and 100% concentration. From Westerdale we had the gruelling climb back up onto Rosedale Head - 400ft up in half a mile is the appetiser for this two-mile ascent - before a return to the peaty track along Cut Road. Crossed by numerous streamlets the trail once again demanded eyes-down full attention and it was only by chance that I glanced up and got my first sighting of the North Sea. What a view! Beyond the patchwork fields of Great Fryup Dale a strip of deep blue heralded our journey's end. It was a great feeling. But it also meant that tomorrow was the last day; that thought tempered our pleasure with regrets.

As evening drew in the setting sun saw us motoring down Glaisdale Rigg, dust clouds billowing out behind. As there are no youth hostels mid-moor we'd booked in at a B&B down in

Glaisdale. It made a welcome change and we spent the evening by the fire swopping trail tales with two lads on the last leg of their coast-to-coast walk.

Wind Down to the Sea

Fully fuelled with a magnificent farmhouse fry-up we set off for the final day in high spirits. Of course, deep in the heart of the dale, we had no hint of the sea ahead but the scent of a journey's end was in the air. We breezed down the lane - passing our two walking companions on the way - keen to kick off on the first of our last bits of off-road; the nettle-clogged bridleway at Carr End. Fitter from six solid days of trekking we found the gritty climb up to Smith's Lane a piece of cake but we nearly caught a car on the serpentine descent through Delves. Too much trail riding had obviously affected our road sense. A quick stop in Grosmont for supplies, and then the big climb of the day to Sleights Moor.

I viewed the little arrows on the map with respect but Aaron was in invincible mood and reckoned it would be a breeze. He was right. We cruised over it. It wasn't effortless though, we shed some sweat. Now our goal was in sight. Robin Hood's Bay seemed a mere stone's throw away. But our coast-to-coast route had a few more miles of trail blazing left in it beginning with more pale-trail cruising at Pike Rigg. A gate beside the A169 marks the jump-off point for eight miles of pure off-road bliss that is not to be missed. With gentle climbs, long, dust-kicking descents and good waymarkers it was dead simple to follow; all we had to do was put the hammer down. A lunch stop on Louven Howe - Filingdales looks really weird this close, especially that large 'speaker box' - then it was back to kicking down the cranks for some prime-time cruising again. At this rate we were in for an early finish. But there's nothing like a couple of missing waymarkers, an invisible trail and a re-route to set you back.

Park Hill, down in Harwood Dale, was where things went awry. As sure as there were little green dashes on the map there was dashed all on the ground. A barbed wire fence barred the way and

*Overleaf (main picture): **The perfect view to end England's finest long-distance off-road route. Inset: Grosmont, terminus for the North Yorkshire Moors steam railway.***

it was nearly an hour before we had it sorted, found a new bridle-gate and were on our way again. Frustration was soon forgotten and we were spinning up Helwath Road, keen to catch sight of the North Sea and our journey's end.

But the sighting came later, rather than sooner. Not until we'd crossed Howdale Moor, reached the radio mast by the Old Scarborough Road and hung a left did we get our first view of Robin Hood's Bay harbour. This was the perfect approach. The village, a huddle of red-tiled rooftops tucked in below the cliffs, was barely two miles away as the crow flies, but we still had a last two-and-a-half-mile off-road run on an old rail route to enjoy.

With the scent of the North Sea in the wind and the cry of gulls in the air we took off, tyres humming on the dry dirt, leaving a trail of dust in our wake. It was a dash for the finish. A blur of black cinders, dappled light and green trees, then suddenly we were surrounded by crowds of trippers wending their way up from a day on the beach. Buckets in hand, toddlers dripping ice-cream and all totally oblivious to the two mud-caked bikers with a 210-mile trek and another coast at their backs.

ROUTE ABBREVIATIONS AND INSTRUCTIONS

The route is split into eight day's of riding, but this is only a guideline. The highlighted villages and landmarks on the maps correspond to key points in the route directions.   A brief description of the day's ride, including parts of the route to watch out for, is provided at the beginning of each day's ride. Overnight stops are suggested, but again, this is only a guideline. The nearest train stations to each day's starting and finishing points are given for anyone wishing to do the route in sections.

The instructions are brief and to the point to make them easy to follow while riding. If in any doubt, always refer to the map and check your compass to ensure you are heading in the right direction. Compass directions are given after each turning.

The following abbreviations have been used:

Turn L : Turn left
Turn R: Turn right
SO: Straight over
X-roads: crossroads
C-road: classified road

Wet weather routes have been given where necessary.

KEY

 Map Orientation

 Technical Information

 Overnight Stops

 Off-Road Code

 Wet weather route

NOTE TO THE MAP SECTION:

The maps used are Ordnance Survey 1:50000 series which have been reduced by 20%. Therefore, one mile is equivalent to one inch and one kilometre to 1.6 cm.
Kilometres:

1 Km   2 Km

Statute miles:

1 m   2 m

MAP 1

DAY 1

ST BEES TO ENNERDALE
17 miles (10 miles off-road)
Summits: Kelton Fell - 835ft.
Closest railway station: St Bees

The Irish Sea's at your back and the North Sea's 125 miles away - as the crow flies. As tyre-treads roll it's 210 miles to the Yorkshire coast and well over half of that's prime-time dirt-tracking.

As with most coast-to-coasters you'll probably be making a late afternoon start and Ennerdale YHA, just over an hour's ride into the mountains, is an ideal first stop. There's nothing technical, just a couple of miles of dirt track to hum along, but if you've had a long journey to St Bees you'll appreciate an easy introduction. Watch those bends on the hill off Kelton Fell!

On the other hand if you're fit and it's morning then the Eskdale YHA, 30 miles away, is well within range. Weather permitting. In a couple of hours you'll be tackling your first technical single-track with Lakeland summits crowding your horizons. Definitely in at the deep end!

Car Park, St Bees Beach	From St Bees beach car park, take C-road (E) towards St Bees for 0.3m. Turn L (NE) for 0.25m to B5345. Go SO (NE) to climb 2m to staggered X-roads. Turn R (E) for 0.6m on C-road down over railway bridge then turn L (N) for 0.1m through estate to dismantled railway rail-path.
Mirehouse, rail-path	Head SE on rail-path, under road and follow for 6m into station yard car park at Rowrah.

OFF-ROAD CODE
Cycle only on permitted rights of way

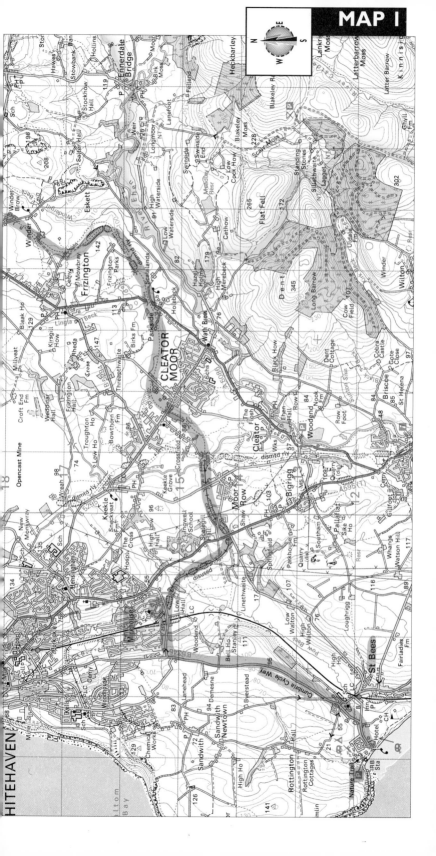

MAP 1

MAP 2

Rowrah, old station	At far end of car park turn R (E), continuing on rail-path for 1m to C-road. Turn L (NE) on C-road to School X-roads then turn R (E) for 0.5m to Kirkland X-roads. Go SO (E) for 1m to T-junction then turn R (SSE) for 1m down steep, zig-zag hill (take care!) to Croasdale.
Croasdale	

Ennerdale YHA	Keep L then R through buildings to head (SE) for Ennerdale. Car park and toilets, by Bowness barrier, are 2m away. Go SO (SE) at barrier for 2.4m on track to Ennerdale YHA. (**Suggested overnight stop**)

DAY 2

ENNERDALE TO ESKDALE
15 miles (13 miles off-road)
Passes: Black Sail - 1800ft; Burnmoor - 990ft.
Nearest train station to Ennerdale: St Bees
Nearest train station to Eskdale: Ravenglass

Don't be fooled by the short distance covered, with Black Sail Pass to climb and a radical descent into Wasdale this section's quite a proving ground. Remember to unweight the bike as much as possible, it's an 850ft carry up to the col, some of it pretty steep. On the descent take on speed with caution, especially on the twists and turns above Gatherstone Beck ford, and don't forget to take account of your pack's extra weight.

Down in Wasdale the becks will be inundated after rain - use the detour route. The Burnmoor crossing is simplified by regular cairns which begin just beyond the wood above Wast Water; not quite bottomless at 250ft but still England's deepest lake. The run down below Boat How features the odd little drop-off here and there plus some rough rubble on the approach to Boot. All in all a great piece of downhilling.

	From YHA turn R (E) on track for 3.5m.
Black Sail Hut	Exit forest at gate. Go SO (ESE) for 0.2m to Black Sail hut.
	Swing R (SE) on single-track bridleway 0.3m to cross stream (boggy here). Path swings R (S then SW) for 0.5m carry on to Black Sail Pass col. It's 2.2m (SW then S) on obvious path to Wasdale Head. The first 0.25m is steep, loose and treacherous.

MAP 3

Wasdale Head On C-road turn R (S) for 0.25. On RH bend go SO (SSE) on bridleway. Ford Lingmell Beck after 0.5m. Continue (SW) past camp-site for 0.2m to cross Lingmell Gill bridge (not Lingmell Beck bridge which is off to the R, near the road).

WET WEATHER ROUTE FROM WASDALE HEAD
On C-road from Wasdale Head turn R (S) for 1m. Turn L (ESE) for 0.2m on track, over Lingmell Beck bridge then swing R to cross Lingmell Gill bridge.

From Lingmell Gill bridge turn L (ESE) for 0.8m on bridleway that swings R (S) (rubbled climb) to a fork, just beyond copse. Keep L (S) for 1.2m up over Maiden Castle Cairn hill, following regular

Burnmoor Tarn Bridge cairns, to footbridge on northern shore of Burnmoor Tarn. Swing R (SSE then SSW) for 2.5m on cairn-marked bridleway that gently climbs flank of Boat How (ignore footpath that veers off L

Boot down into the Whillan Beck valley) then descends to track to Eskdale Mill at Boot.

Go SO (S) on C-road, over bridge, 0.2m to T-junction. Turn L (ENE) for 1.25m to Eskdale YHA.

Eskdale YHA **(Suggested overnight stop)**

DAY 3

ESKDALE TO TOWN END
27 miles (16 miles off-road)
Passes: Harter Fell - 1165ft; Brown Pike (Walna Scar) - 2000ft; The Hundreds - 820ft.
Nearest railway station to Eskdale: Ravenglass.
Nearest railway station to Town End: Windermere

Beware the Duddon step-stones, they're dangerous after heavy rain, and use the detour if needed. The Walna Scar Road - an ancient packhorse by-way - is a well-established, premium grade mountain bike route. The descent to Coniston is very broken in parts, precipitous and not so much fast as breakneck. Take care. The road bends into Coniston are also worthy of respect. Bar a series of water runnels to hop on Loughrigg Terrace, Coniston sees the end of the day's technicalities.

Ambleside is ideal for a bit of R&R, re-stock and has the best bike shops on the route. Bike Treks and Gyhllside Cycles (see page 92).

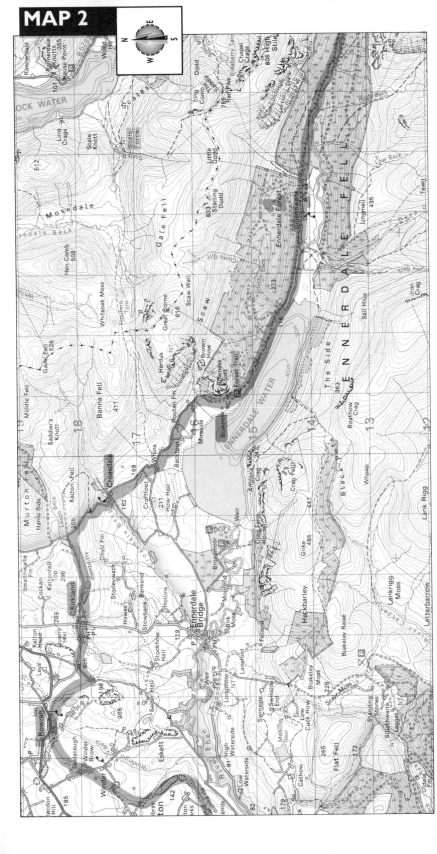

MAP 2

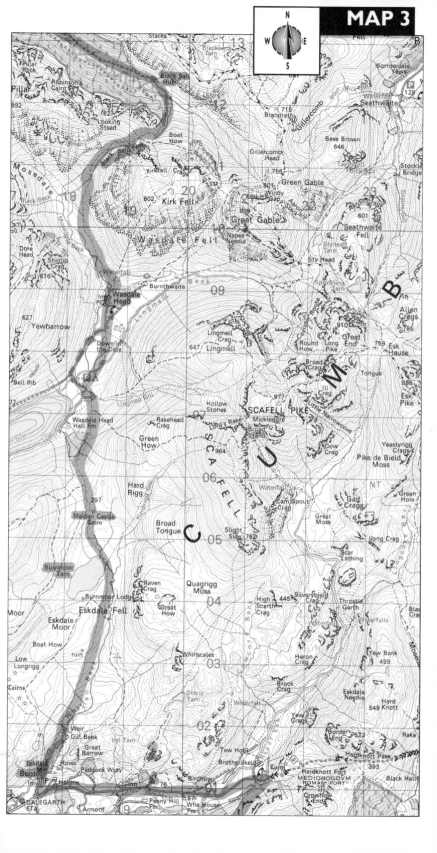

MAP 3

MAP 4

Eskdale YHA From YHA entrance turn L (E) for 1.3m on C-road to just past cattle grid. Turn R on bridleway, over Hardknott Gill, up through two gates.
Path climbs (SW, S then SSE) for 1.4m round Harter Fell to signpost at forest edge. Go SO (SE) for 0.35m of mud, root and boulder strewn path to forest track terminus. Ignore bridleway down to the R and follow track (SE) for 0.75m to Y-junction.

Grassguards Ford Take hairpin R (SW) for 0.5m to Grassguards Farm ford on zig-zag track where you turn L then R at the next two T-junctions. These follow in quick succession.
Don't cross river but turn L (E) downstream on tricky single-track for 0.6m, round Crag, and down steep descent to step-stones. Cross River Duddon and turn R (SSE) for 220yds to C-road. Single-track bridleway isn't as obvious as the parallel footpath but both end up on the road. R (S) for 0.5m to Tarn Beck Bridge.

 WET WEATHER ROUTE FROM Y-JUNCTION BY FOREST TRACK
At Y-junction go SO (E then SE) for 0.5m to T-junction. Hairpin turn R (SE) past Birks house on bridleway to bridge to C-road 0.5m away. Turn R (S) for 2m on C-road to Tarn Beck Bridge. (This detour is also much easier.)

Tarn Beck bridge Go SO (SE) for 100yds up to Y-junction. Hairpin L (N) for 0.6m on unclassified road to T-junction with unclassified track just before crossing stream. Turn R (E) for 0.8m up Walna Scar Road (the unclassified track) to gate. Go SO (SE) for 75yds up Walna Scar then turn L (ENE) for 0.5m on track to col below Brown Pike. At 1985ft it's the Coast-to-Coast's highest pass. Well done!

Brown Pike col Carry SO (ESE) for 2.2m (very steep, loose and rocky in places. Take care!) on obvious track to beginning of metalled lane, ignoring paths descending off R to Tranearth. These lead off about 1m from the col. Go SO (E) for 1m on unclassified road (take care, bends down to Coniston are steep and sharp!), keeping R on edge of town, to A593 at Coniston.

Coniston Turn L (N) for 1.7m on A593, through town

MAP 5

centre, to Y-junction. L (NNW) for 1.25m on C-road to High Tiberthwaite.

High Tiberthwaite

Go through farmyard and exit via gate to R. Go 1.25m on obvious bridleway track (E) to ford at Little Langdale keeping R at first fork (0.5m) and L at second (0.6m).

Little Langdale Ford

Go SO (N) for 0.4m on unclassified road, using bridge (ford is deep and wide!), up to T-junction. Turn L (WNW) for 0.15m on C-road to T-junction with track.

Turn R (NNE) for 1.2m on obvious track, keeping R at forks at 0.6m (just after gate on edge of wood) and 1m respectively, to Y-junction with C-road at Elterwater.

Elterwater

Go SO (N) for 0.5m to B5343 X-roads, keeping SO (N) at fork in village centre. Go SO (N) on C-road for 0.2m up to T-junction. Turn R (E) for 0.75m climbing past YHA to Y-junction.

Keep L (N) for 150yds down to take bridleway off R (NE) for 250yds to tricky ford on Loughrigg Terrace.

Loughrigg Terrace

Go SO (ENE) for 0.5m. Path zig-zags down alongside wood. Go SO (E) for 0.5m on Rydal Water's shore then keep R, up to gate.

Rydal Water

Go SO (E) for 0.4m on unclassified road to T-junction. Turn L then R on A591 to go into Ambleside centre otherwise turn R (S) on C-road for 1.6m to T-junction. Turn L (E) towards Ambleside across bridge on A593. Watch out for one-way system now. Immediately L (NNE) again for 0.2m to T-junction. Turn R (E) for 220yds to T-junction. Turn R (S) on A591 for 0.25m to Y-junction at Waterhead.

Waterhead

Hairpin turn L (NNE) for 80yds. Hairpin turn R (SSE) for 1.25m on bridleway to High Skelghyll farm. On the way keep R at first fork (0.1m), L at second fork (0.5m), climb L then R across Stencher Beck (0.6m) and stop at Jenkin Crag (0.8m) for view.

Go SO (ESE) on through farm 220yds to RH bend. Attend to signposts! Quit drive for single-track bridleway and go SO (E) for 0.2m then swing R (SSE) on track for 0.6m as it swings L (E) to T-junction. Turn R (SSE) for 0.3m to T-junction with C-road. Turn L (NE) for 80yds then fork R (ENE)

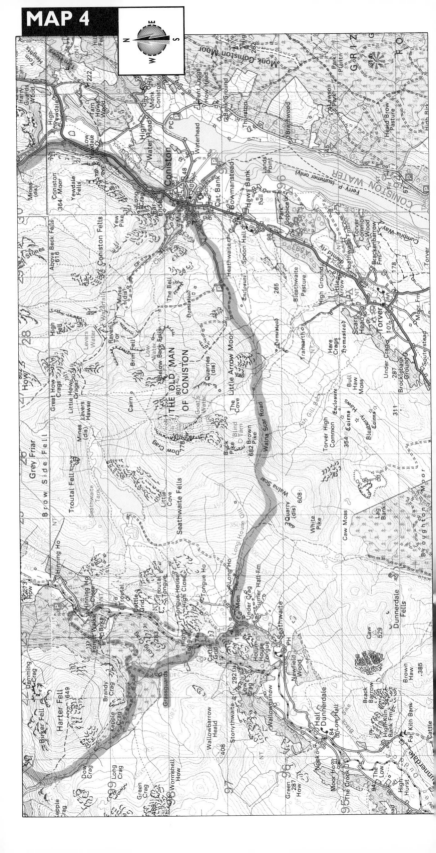

MAP 4

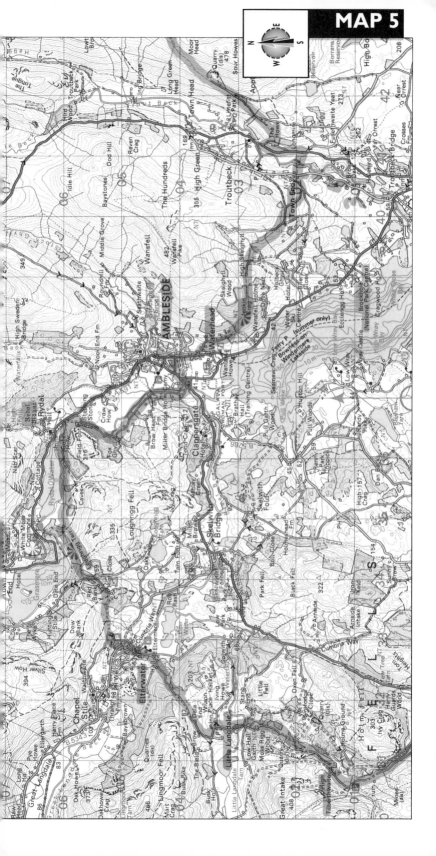

MAP 5

MAP 6

Town end 	on bridleway track for 150 yds to the Windermere YHA C-road/bridleway X-roads at Town End. (For Windermere YHA turn R for 0.5m). (**Suggested Overnight Stop**)

DAY 4

TOWN END TO KIRKBY STEPHEN
36 miles (19 miles off-road)
Passes: Garburn - 1475ft; Stile End - 1160ft;
Mosedale - 1640ft; High Wether - 1600ft.
Summits: Bank Moor - 1055ft.
Nearest railway station to Town End: Windermere
Nearest railway station to Kirkby Stephen: Kirkby Stephen

Although it's a long leg and there's a fair bit of climbing, by now you'll be acclimatised to day-on-day biking with a pack and it'll be easier than it looks on paper.

Kentmere is a small, scattered hamlet on the north shore of a silted up lake. Bear in mind that the tea rooms only open in the afternoon. Route finding over Mosedale can be tricky in foul weather - use a compass to find first the gate south of Selside Brow then the Cottage. The Swindale route uses **NWWA** roads for which we have permissive access - follow any detours etc that may be posted by the **NWWA**.

Shap is the best mid-ride stop. It's well known for high grade stone but before the huge quarries came the White Canons who founded the now ruined abbey in 1199. Of more interest to Coast-to-Coasters is the chippy.

The road ride to Kirkby is punctuated by farmland off-roading. Take

Windermere YHA **The Howe** **MAP 6** **Kentmere** **Stile End**	From YHA go back to X-roads at Town End and turn R (ESE) onto bridleway for 0.25m, crossing bridge, and on up to A592. Turn L (N) for 0.4m to turn R (SE) onto bridleway track. Climb, round LH bend after 200 yds, for 0.4m to X-roads. Go SO (NE) for 1.8m to summit at Garburn Pass. Descend (E) on rocky track for 1.25m to meet end of C-road at Kentmere. Keep SO (S) for 0.4m, past church, to T-junction then turn L (ENE) for 0.2m up to another T-junction. Turn L (N) for 0.6m then turn R (E) onto bridleway track (steep and rocky on far side of pass) for 1.2m, passing farm, to T-junction. Keep L (NE), through gate, for 0.5m descent to Sadgill

MAP 7

Sadgill Bridge

Bridge. Turn L (N) for 2m up track, just beyond gate, to signpost. Next section is boggy and indistinct. Fork R (NNE) for 0.3m, then path swings R (NE) by old quarry workings for 200yds then R (E) again for 250 yds to gate. Beyond gate keep SO (ENE) for 0.7m on more defined path to ruins of Mosedale Cottage.
Continue (ENE) for 0.35m on track and cross ford.

Mosedale Cottage

 WET WEATHER ROUTE FROM T-JUNCTION AT STILE END
Quit track and keep SO (ENE) for 2m on single-track to Swindale Head farm. (The first 0.5m that contours the lower slopes of Howes is faint and the drop down Nabs Moor spur is steep.) Go SO (NE) for 2.7m on unclassified road to X-roads. Take hairpin R (S) for 2m on permissive NWWA road to X-roads then fork L (SE) for 1.4m, via Keld, to T-junction, Shap. Turn R (NE) for 0.25m to A6 at Shap. Turn R (S) for 0.2m to T-junction with C-road to Crosby.

From Mosedale ford track swings R (SE) then L (ENE) for 0.5m to cross bridge. Climb zig-zag route up fell on track then continue (ENE) for 3.25m above Wet Sleddale to sharp R turn by wall (section on col, south of High Wether Howes, is tricky to follow; ignore R turns down into valley). Keep R (SE) for 1m through farm to join C-road at Thorney Bank. Turn L (NE) for 0.6m to A6. Turn L (N) for 1.7m to T-junction with C-road to Crosby.

Shap
T-junction

Take C-road R (E) 4.25m to Crosby Ravensworth. At T-junction turn L (NE) for 0.15m, past church, to T-junction. Turn R (E) for 0.1m on unclassified road then turn R (S) at fork for 0.5m to Bank Head.

OFF-ROAD CODE
Give way to horse riders and walkers

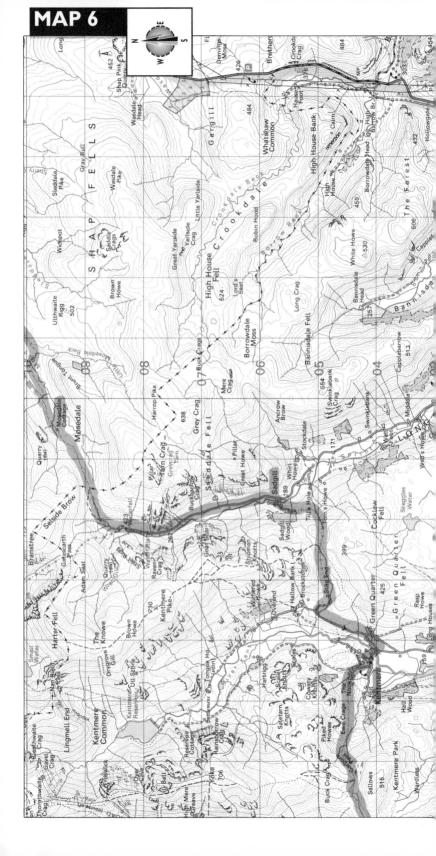

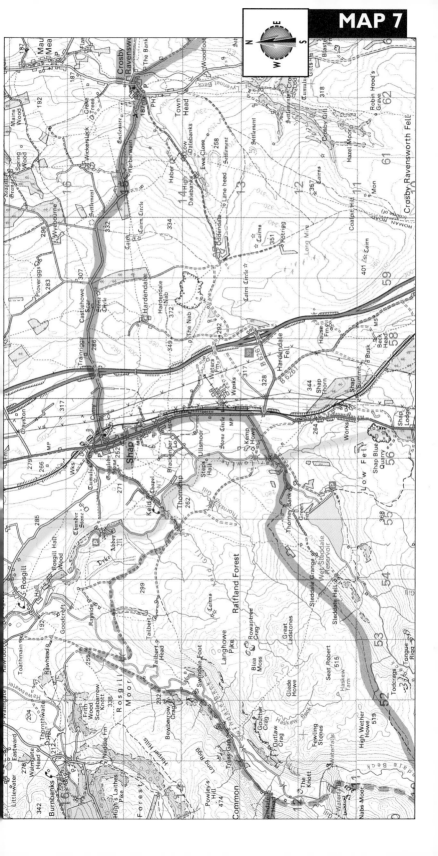

MAP 7

MAP 8

Go SO (SSE) on bridleway across pasture for 0.8m to B6260 at Bank Moor. Turn R (SE) for 0.4m to T-junction.

WET WEATHER ROUTE FROM BANK HEAD
At Bank Head turn L (ENE) for 0.6m on drive through farm to B6260 then turn R (S) for 1m to T-junction.

Bank Moor	Turn L (SSE) for 2m on C-road towards Gt Ashby. Turn R (SE) for 1m on bridleway track to Maisongill farm.
Maisongill	Go SO (ESE) through gate following waymarked route for 0.8m across fields (please detour round crops if necessary and do not frighten stock) to unclassified road at Ashby Grange.
Ashby Grange	Keep R (ENE) for 300yds to bridleway off R. Follow waymarked bridleway (E) 1.1m (ziz-zag detour at 0.6m) to C-road just north of Whygill
Whygill Head, X-roads	Head farm. Turn R (S) for 50yds to X-roads. Keep L (E) for 3m, following signs for Kirkby
Soulby	Stephen, to Soulby.

MAP 9

In village centre turn R (S) for 2.2m to A685 in Kirkby Stephen. Turn R (S) for 0.2m to Kirkby Stephen YHA in chapel on R. (**Suggested Overnight Stop**)

DAY 5

KIRKBY STEPHEN TO GRINTON
30 miles (18 miles off-road)
Passes: Pennine Watershed (Molds Hill) - 1600ft; Crackpot - 1200ft; Apedale Head - 1790ft.
Summits: Tan Hill - 1790ft; Greets Hill - 1675ft.
Nearest railway station to Kirkby Stephen: Kirkby Stephen
Nearest railway station to Grinton: North Allerton

Once again take note of recent rainfalls before setting out to ford the Belah river beyond Wrenside. Take the road alternative if there's been a recent deluge. Don't forget to drop in at the Tan Hill Inn to celebrate getting halfway. Tan Hill also marks the start of a short section in common with the Pennine Way. Being peat trail it's subject to erosion in bad conditions and the road makes an easy alternative. It's fast too!

Down in Swaledale the Punchbowl Inn at Low Row, on the B6270 opposite Low Houses, has a mountain bike centre if you need supplies.

MAP 9

Kirkby
Stephen YHA
Winton

Rookby

Wrenside

From YHA turn L (N) on A685 for 0.25m through town to T-junction. Turn R (NE) for 0.5m on C-road towards Winton. At T-junction turn L (N) for 1m to Winton then turn R (E) at T-junction for 3.8m (ignore L turn at 1.25m, Rookby) to end of C-road. Keep SO (ESE) for 0.7m on bridleway track, past Wrenside farm, to barn. Keep L (ENE to NE) alongside wall for 250yds to ford River Belah.

WET WEATHER ROUTE FROM ROOKBY
At Rookby turn L (NNW) for 0.2m to T-junction then turn R (E) for 3m to T-junction (If you really want an unclassified route then turn R at 2.3m, on bridleway, to High Ewebank and on to River Belah ford). Turn R (SW) for 5.5m, beginning with a steep climb, to Tan Hill Inn.

Woofergill

From River Belah ford turn R (ESE) upstream for 0.3m when path zig-zags up, past derelict Woofergill barn, to forest edge. Continue (SE) for 0.1m onto moor via bridle-gate ('Tan Hill Inn' C-road is now 0.5m away, almost due E of gate, but undefined bridleway route heads SE for circuitous 1m loop to road.). To follow bridleway route continue (SE) for 0.3m across moor then turn L (ENE) for 0.4m to fellside and finally climb 0.1m to C-road. Turn R (SE) for 2.5m to Tan Hill Inn (England's E/W watershed is crossed about 2m from Inn).

OFF-ROAD CODE
Do not ride in such a manner that you are a danger to others

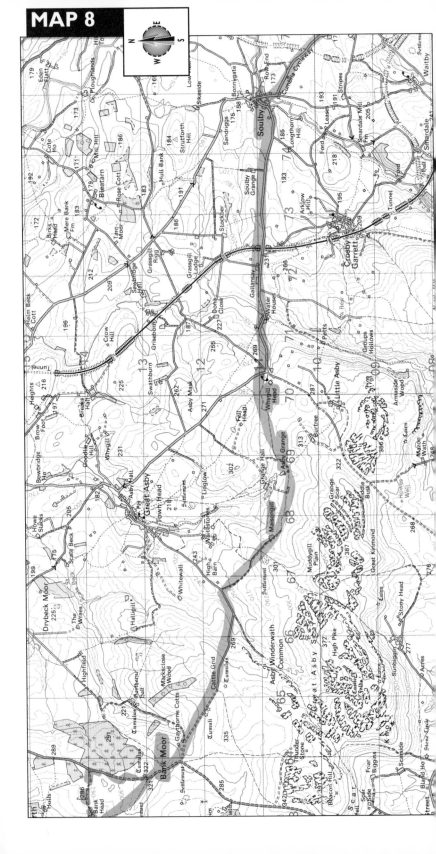

MAP 8

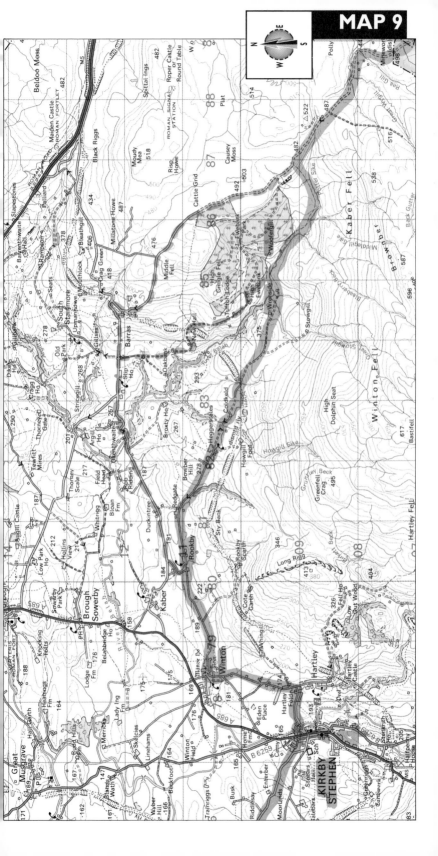

MAP 9

MAP 10

Tan Hill Inn Turn R (S) onto obvious track - it's the Pennine Way and can be busy with hikers - for 0.4m ascent of Tan Hill. Keep SO (SSW) on less defined, often boggy single-track for 1.25m.

Low Frith Pennine Way now swings L (SSE) for 2.2m, past Low Frith, to East Stonesdale farm.

WET WEATHER ROUTE FROM TAN HILL
From just before Tan Hill turn R (S) for 3.25m on C-road to T-junction with unclassified road on sharp RH bend. Turn L (E) for 0.6m to East Stonesdale farm.

East Stonesdale Farm Go SO (SSE) on track, through farmyard 150yds down hill to swing L, off the Pennine Way and across bridge above falls. Keep SO (ESE) on track for 0.75m to fork then keep R (SE) for 2m roller-coaster track to unclassified road at Ramps Holme.

Ramps Holme Continue SO (SE) for 1.4m to T-junction then turn R (S) on C-road for 0.5m, down

Ivelet through Ivelet, across bridge to B6270. Turn L (E) for 0.5m to Satron.

Satron, B6270 Keep SO (E) for 0.5m then, on LH bend, go SO (E) for 20yds on C-road then fork L (ENE) onto unclassified track for 1.75m to C-road.

MAP 11

Turn L (NE) for 0.6m, ignoring L turn across river, to Low Houses.

Low Houses Turn R (SE) then swing L (E) for 0.5m, steep and rough climb to C-road then turn R (SSW) to continue 1m climb to bridleway track off L (SSE). Climb for 1.3m (as gradient eases track peters out and path swings E across streamlets) to gate and spoil heap at Apedale Head.

Apedale Head Keep spoil heap to R and swing L (NE) then R (SE) on more obvious, but boggy track, for 2.25m to X-roads at Dents Houses. Turn L (N) for 1m up bridleway track, through butts, to gate.

Greets Hill Go SO (NE), past Greets Hill's twin cairns, for 0.75m down through mine workings to C-road then turn L (NNE) for 1.2m and turn R (E) on track for 0.1m to Grinton Lodge YHA. (**Suggested overnight stop**)

MAP 11

WET WEATHER ROUTE FROM LOW HOUSES

At Low Houses keep L (NE) for 1.5m on unclassified track to C-road. Go SO (E) for 0.75m, ignoring L turn across river, then turn L (NE) onto single-track bridleway for 50yds to go through bridle-gate into meadows below Stubbing Farm. Fork R (NE) on waymarked, gated bridleway for 1.8m down to and alongside River Swale to C-road at Swale Hall. Turn L (E) for 0.3m to Grinton. Turn R (S) for 0.6m climb to Grinton Lodge YHA.

DAY 6

GRINTON TO OSMOTHERLEY
33 miles (13 miles off-road)
Summits: Marrick - 1035ft; Croft How - 985ft.
Nearest Railway Station to both Grinton and Osmotherley: North Allerton

This'll be your first day without wild country to cross. It's also one that frequently coincides with the other C-to-C so look out for over-packed pedestrians and follow the bridleway waymarkers.

Richmond is the main town on the route. If you need bike supplies the major MTB centre is just out of town on the Gallowfields industrial estate. Of course you should visit the castle and enjoy one of the many eateries that populate the compact centre.

Another C-to-C pub stop is at Danby Whiske. A pretty, brick-built

Grinton Lodge YHA

From YHA, turn R (N) for 0.7m descent to T-junction with B6270. Go SO (N) for 0.3m to Low Fremington. Turn R (E) onto C-road for 0.5m then fork R (ESE) for 1m on unclassified road to Marrick Abbey farm.

OFF-ROAD CODE
Take all litter with you

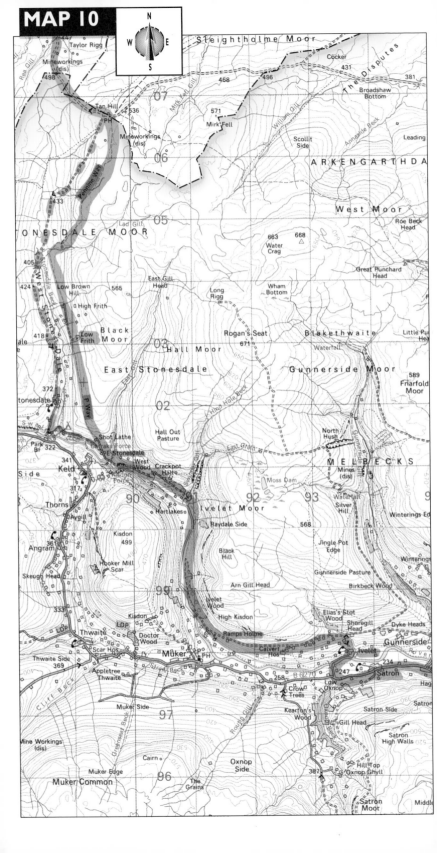

MAP 10

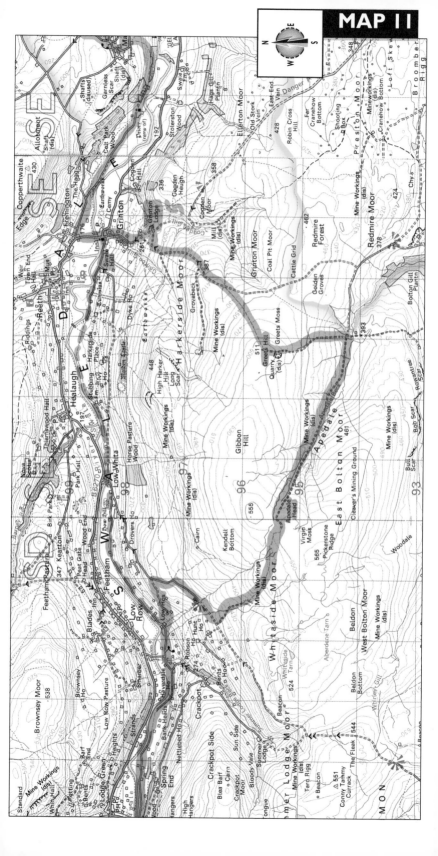

MAP 11

MAP 12

Continue (ESE) past buildings, onto track, for 0.75m to fork. Keep L (N) through gate up walled track for 0.1m to T-junction. Turn R (E) then immediately L (N) on unclassified road for 0.1m into Marrick.

Marrick
Turn R (ENE) for 250yds round to C-road T-junction. Turn R (ENE) for 0.5m to Nun Cote Nook farm track.

Nun Cote Nook Farm
Turn R (E) on bridleway for 0.6m, keeping farm buildings to your L, to fork. Keep R (ESE) up hill for 0.4m up to and along boundary then swing L (ENE) 0.2m down by small quarry to farm track. Turn R (E) 50yds to gate. Keep SO (E) for 0.3m down to Low Oxque farm.

Low Oxque
Turn L (NE) on bridleway track for 0.7m to C-road. Turn L (NW) for 1m to T-junction then turn R (NE) through Marske.

Marske
Continue (E) for 1.25m and take hairpin R (S) onto bridleway track for 1m to West Applegarth.

Applegarth
Follow track around R (S) side of buildings, then turn R (SE) round barn and continue 0.5m to East Applegarth farm. Bridleway now swings uphill (NE) for a few yards then turns R (E) for 2.2m then through Whitecliffe Wood 2.2m, down through woods, on unclassified track/road to the A6108 in Richmond.

Richmond
Follow A6108 (E) through town (Signed 'Darlington') for 0.6m to fork with B6271, 'Brompton' road. Fork R (ESE) on B6271 for 4m to Brompton-on-Swale

 OFF-ROAD CODE
Keep erosion to a minimum and do not skid

MAP 13

Brompton-on-Swale	Fork L (ENE), still on B6271, for 0.4m to X-roads. Cross A6136 and continue SO (E) for 1.7m to T-junction then turn R (S), towards Bolton-on-Swale still on B6271, for 1.4m, passing through Bolton, to Ellerton X-roads.
Ellerton	Turn L (NE) for 3.5m on C-road that meanders E to Streetlam. Keep L (NE) for 250yds then turn R (E) for 1.6m to Danby Wiske for obligatory C-to-C pub stop.

OFF-ROAD CODE
Be courteous and considerate to others

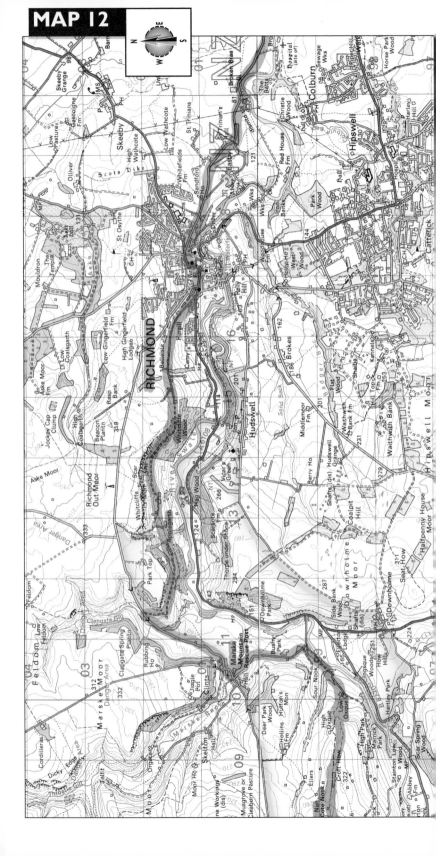

MAP 12

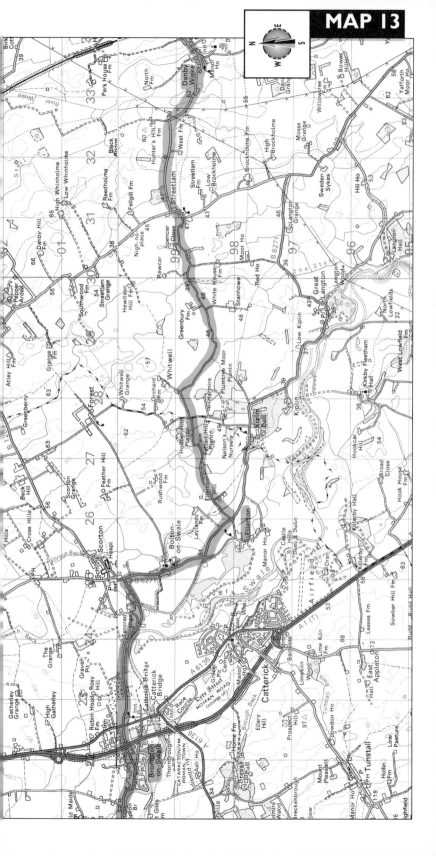

MAP 13

MAP 14

Danby Wiske	Keep straight on (ENE) through village for 1.3m to T-junction (easy to miss!) then turn L (ENE) for 0.6m to A167. Turn L (N) then almost immediately R (E) on C-road for 1.7m to X-roads in the centre of Brompton.
Brompton	Go SO (SE) to A684 then turn L (NE) for 4m to roundabout on A1. Follow signs for 'Osmotherley'.
Osmotherley	Keep SO (E) on C-road for 1m into Osmotherley village. At T-junction turn L (N) for 0.5m then fork R (NNE) down to Osmotherley YHA. (**Suggested overnight stop**)

DAY 7

OSMOTHERLEY TO GLAISDALE
31 miles (24 miles off-road)
Passes: Stoney Wicks (Crossletts) - 1085ft.
Summits: Beacon Hill (Scarth Wood Moor) - 980ft;
Round Hill (Urra Moor) - 1490ft; Burton Howe - 1390ft;
Baysdale Moor - 1290ft; Rosedale Head - 1355ft;
Glaisdale Rigg - 1070ft.
Nearest Railway Station to Osmotherley: North Allerton
Nearest Railway Station to Glaisdale: Glaisdale

If you were to steam due east across the North York Moors you'd be talking real hard work as you cross six dales! Instead we turn north, tread round the rim of the Cleveland Hills and drop into Glaisdale. With a dip in and out of Westerdale on the way.

   Once again, if the weather's been wet, alternative routes detour round the slip-spots of East Bank Plantation and the off-road climb out of Westerdale. It'll also be real boggy on the Cut Road so warn your B&B hosts that you're a dirty lot when compared to the normal coast-to-coasters. We saw the North Sea from here for the first time but you can get a glimpse much earlier in the day. I won't say where, that's a moment for you to enjoy.

   Navigation is straightforward but proceed with care round Crossletts, in East Bank Plantation and amid the numerous tracks on Urra Moor. Baysdale, because it's fast, is another place that may see you off-road and off-route.

Osmotherley YHA	From YHA turn L (SSW) for 0.1m on C-road towards Osmotherley then take hairpin R (N) for 1.2m on unclassified road to LH bend. Keep SO (NNE) onto bridleway track for 0.3m to gate. Go through, veer R (NE) down track for 0.6m across Scarth Wood Moor then turn R (SE) for 250yds to C-road.
Scarth Wood Moor	

MAP 15

Huthwaite Green

Turn L (N) for 250 yds to gated track into wood, on Cleveland Way, for 0.5m to fork then turn L (NE) for 0.2m down to single-track bridleway off R. Turn R (E), on Cleveland Way, for 0.6m. Still on Cleveland Way turn L (NE) for 0.2m, across field, to unclassified road. Turn L (NE) for 0.3m to T-junction by Huthwaite Green. Here we leave the Cleveland Way.

Scugdale Hall

Turn R (E) on unclassified road for 1.75m to Scugdale Hall.

Continue SO (E) for 0.1m then turn L (ENE), through gate onto unclassified track (single-track in places) for 0.5m up to moor gate on horizon. Go SO (NE) for 0.2m. Keep to left of boundary. Trail swings gently R (E) for 0.3m down field to gate. Keep SO (E) into sunken lane

Crossletts

past Crossletts Farms for 0.3m to Raisdale Mill. Zig-zag through mill buildings to C-road. Turn R (SE) for 1.5m to B1257 at Chop Gate.

Chop Gate

Turn L (NNE) for 0.4m to Seave Green T-junction. Turn R (ENE) on C-road then almost immediately turn R (E), across ford, and SO up track for 0.3m then fork L (ENE) on bridleway for 250yds round L (N) side of East Bank farm buildings. Go through gate on the R and turn L (E) for 250yds up track to gate at corner of East Bank Plantation.

Turn L (E) up single-track, at first on forest edge then up into trees, for 0.2m. Path swings R (SSE) for 0.1m then veers L (E) 30yds up to gate. (Next climb can be very boggy.) Go through gate, keep L (NNE) for 0.5m on obvious track to T-junction.

WET WEATHER ROUTE FROM B1257
At B1257 turn R (ENE) through Seave Green for 0.3m to LH bend by Bilsdale Hall. Turn R (SE) then bridleway turns L (ENE) round the Hall for 0.75m climb to T-junction.

Coming from East Bank Plantation, turn R (NE) for 1.25m on obvious track to re-join Cleveland Way near triangulation pillar.

OFF-ROAD CODE
Wear a helmet

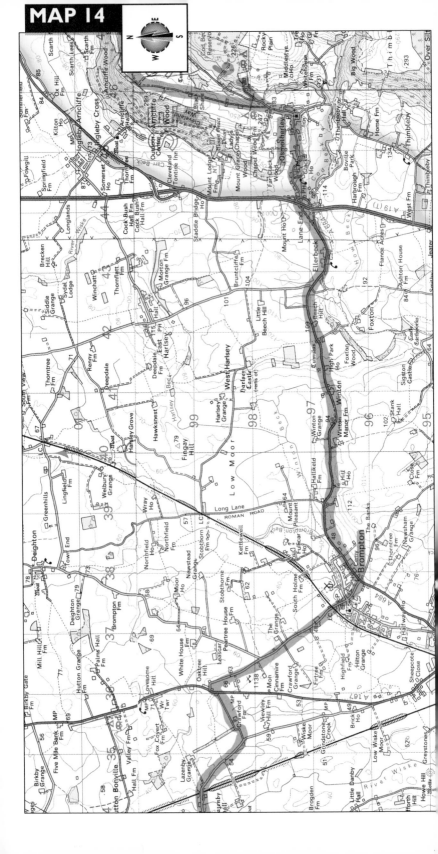

MAP 14

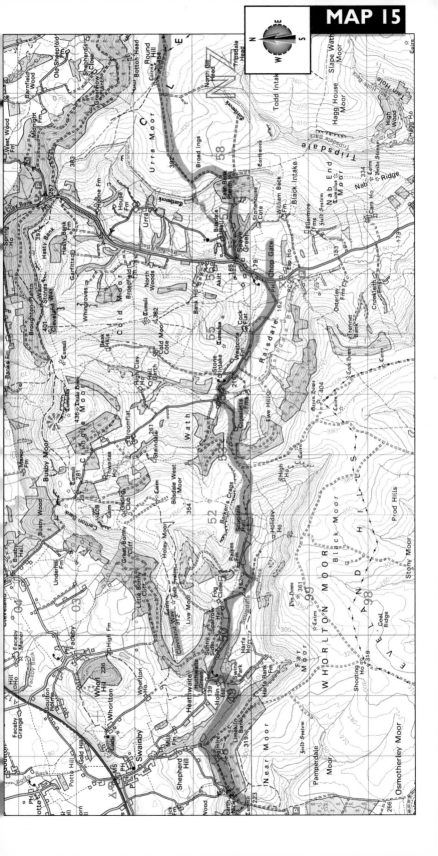

MAP 15

MAP 16

Track swings R (ESE then E) for 1.5m to X-roads. Ignore side turnings. Still on Cleveland Way turn sharp L (NNW) for 1.3m on track then turn R (NE), off the Cleveland Way and onto single-track bridleway for 100yds onto Burton Howe summit.

Burton Howe Go SO (NE) for 0.6m on shooting track then swing R (E) for 0.1m down to T-junction. Turn R (SSE)

Armouth Wath for 0.4m to derelict building (Armouth Wath). Turn L (ESE) for 0.1m, across stream on footbridge, up steep, zig-zag single-track onto Baysdale Moor. Continue (ENE) for 1.4m, path turns to track, to T-junction then turn L (NNW) for 1.1m to X-roads on forest edge. Turn R (NE) on single-track alongside trees for 0.1m to gate. On moor turn R (SE) on single track for 0.5m that swings L (E then NE) down to cross footbridge. Climb up onto Great Hograh Moor.

Great Hograh Moor Continue (SE then E) on obvious single-track for 1.25m to unclassified road. Turn L (NNE) for 0.25m to T-junction then turn sharp R (SSE) on C-road for 1.1m, through Westerdale, to T-

Westerdale junction.

Turn L (ENE) for 0.1m then turn R (S) for 0.5m to

Broad Gate Farm Broad Gate Farm to join bridleway. (Remember to close the gates you have to open between here and Dale Head.)

Dale Head Go SO (SE) for 0.5m to Dale Head then continue (ESE) for 0.4m up to C-road Y-junction and turn R (S) for 1.5m climb on C-road to Rosedale Head T-junction.

WET WEATHER ROUTE FROM WESTERDALE
From Westerdale continue SO (S) for 2.5m climb to T-junction then turn R (S) for 0.1m to next T-junction on Rosedale Head.

Rosedale Head Turn L (ENE) for 1.5m to T-junction then turn L (N) for 0.5m and turn R (E) onto bridleway track for 2.3m, past Trough House building and round

Trough House boggy head of Great Fryup Dale, to C-road.

OFF-ROAD CODE
Be self-sufficient and make sure your bike is safe to ride

MAP 17

Keep L (N) on C-road for 1.1m to Y-junction with unclassified track.

Glaisedale Rigg
Keep R (NE) down Glaisdale Rigg for 1.8m, ignoring side turnings (unless you are B&B'ing in Glaisdale valley in which case use one of the tracks/bridleways off R. These occur every 0.5m or so), to junction by pool.

Glaisdale
Keep L (N) for 0.7m on bridleway to C-road at High Leas. Turn R (E) for 0.5m to T-junction in Glaisdale. (**Suggested overnight stop**)

DAY 8

GLAISDALE TO ROBIN HOOD'S BAY
25 miles (15 miles off-road)
Summits: Egton Grange - 720ft; Sleights Moor - 945ft; Louven Howe 980ft; Beacon Howes - 870ft.
Nearest Railway Station to Glaisdale: Glaisdale
Nearest Railway Station to Robin Hood's Bay: Whitby

Last day and the least - so far as effort and off-road expertise is concerned. But that's not to say the riding's inferior. Grosmont is the en-route tourist hot-spot. It is the TV series *Heartbeat*'s major location and features two railway stations. One for British Rail the other for the North York Railway and, if you're into locos, railway memorabilia are on show in the engine sheds.

If it's late summer you'll spend the last leg coursing through a sea of purple heather on honey-coloured tracks. Tracks that hark back to early man's first travels across the moors. In stark contrast to those ancient waymarkers, the stone crosses, are the ludicrous and disproportionate forms of the Fylingdales Early Warning System. Will they be there at the end of the next millenia I wonder?

Between Brown Hill and Park Hill be sure to follow the bridleway signs. The Woodland Trust owns the woods below Park Hill which means that the land is cared for - please respect that, ride light and leave no sign of your passing.

Finally Robin Hood's Bay. Not only is it one of the most popular tourist stop-offs, it's a mecca for geography students so we're talking folk thicker than fleas on a badger's back. With extreme care and providential trail skills you'll make the harbour slip, dip those tyres in the North Sea and wonder how all those miles slipped past so easily.

Keeping L (S then SE) at next two forks continue 0.6m and turn R (E), just before garage at Carr End,

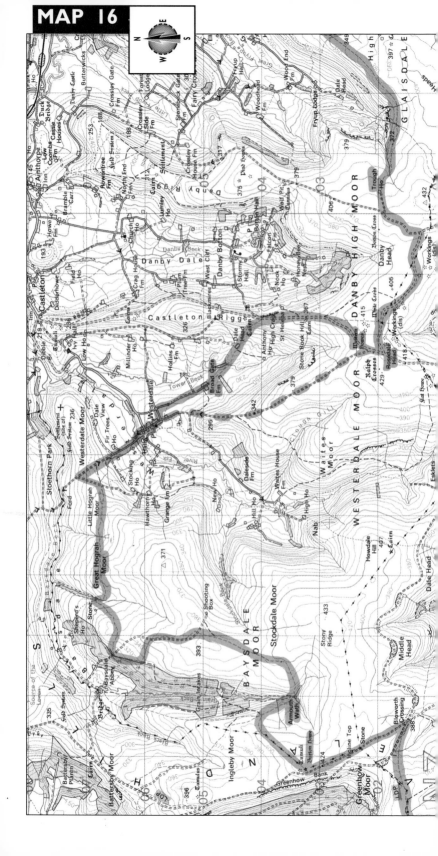

MAP 16

MAP 17

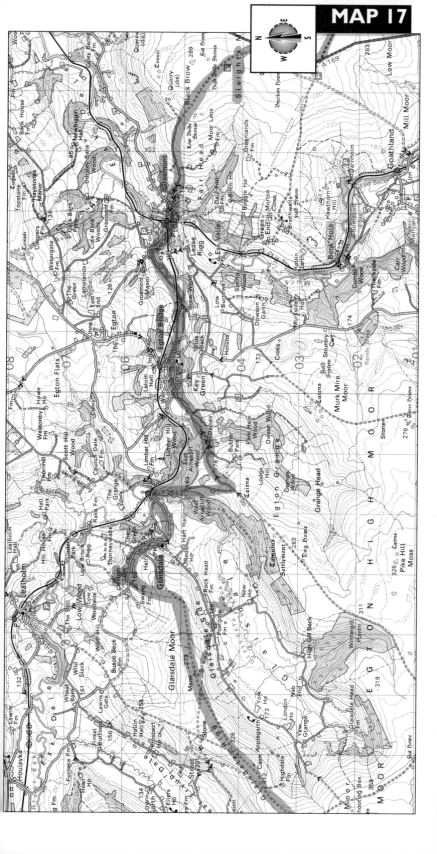

MAP 18

onto bridleway single-track. Go down across footbridge,

swing R (S) for 0.8m up through Arncliff Wood to C-road. Turn L (NE) on C-road for

Egton Bridge

1.7m (beware! Sharp bends) to cross Egton Bridge and then turn R (E) onto permissive, Egton Manor track, for 1.5m to C-road. Turn R (S) for 0.3m to level-crossing in Grosmont.

Grosmont

Keep SO (E) for 300yds up to fork then turn R (ESE) for 300yds to T-junction and

MAP 18

R (ESE) for 2m climb over

Sleights Moor

Sleights Moor to A169 and views towards Robin Hood's Bay. Turn R (SSW) for 0.75m to bridleway gate on the L. Turn L (SE) onto track for 1.5m to fork on York Cross Rigg.

York Cross Rigg

Turn R (S) for 1.8m climb, through gate on Foster Howes Rigg to W side of fence, to triangulation pillar at Louven Howe.

Louven Howe

Continue SO (SE) for 220yds to junction, keep L (SE) for 0.6m to fork and turn R (ESE) for 1.5m descent to gate. Go SO (E) for 1.2m, first alongside fence then on track round Brown Hill,

OFF-ROAD CODE
Avoid livestock, crops and machinery or, if not possible, keep contact to a minimum

MAP 19

Brown Hill to bridleway signpost on the L, just as track straightens. Turn L (ENE) for 0.3m, keeping fence on your L, to gate and track beyond. Turn R (SSE) for 0.3m to T-junction then turn L (ENE) for 0.3m to bridle-gate on the R (just before Park Hill house).

Turn R (due SSE) for 0.5m on bridleway, on remains of track at first, to bridle-gate into wood. Go through gate (NE) down narrow track for 0.1m, over bridge then track swings R (SSE) for 0.1m to field. Turn L (NE) for 0.2m, first across field then on track, to C-road at Chapel Farm.

WET WEATHER ROUTE FROM PARK HILL
At T-junction before Park Hill go SO (S) to T-junction, then L (SE) on unclassified road over Low North Beck to Y-junction. Hairpin L (NW) on C-road and follow road up to Chapel Farm.

Chapel Farm Turn L (N) for 1.8m to A171 then turn L (NW) for 1.1m to take Cook House track

Cook House off R (NE) for 0.2m to junction. Fork R (ENE) on bridleway for 1.8m, keeping SO (ENE) at 0.1m then veering L (ENE) at 1m, to C-road by TV mast on Beacon Howes.

Turn L (NW) for 1m down to take track off L (W) for 0.4m to T-junction. Turn R (N) for 0.1m, zig-zagging past buildings, to dismantled railway path.

Robin Hood's Bay Good views of Robin Hood's Bay. Turn L (W) for 1m, then it's a quick L/R on road and back to rail path for final 1.75m of off-road to C-road. Turn R (NE) for 0.3m to T-junction and turn R (S) for 0.4m and the final descent to Robin Hood's Bay beach.

Boggle Hole YHA Congratulations! Turn R (S) along shore for 0.5m to Boggle Hole YHA if you're hostelling.

OFF-ROAD CODE
Take special care on country roads

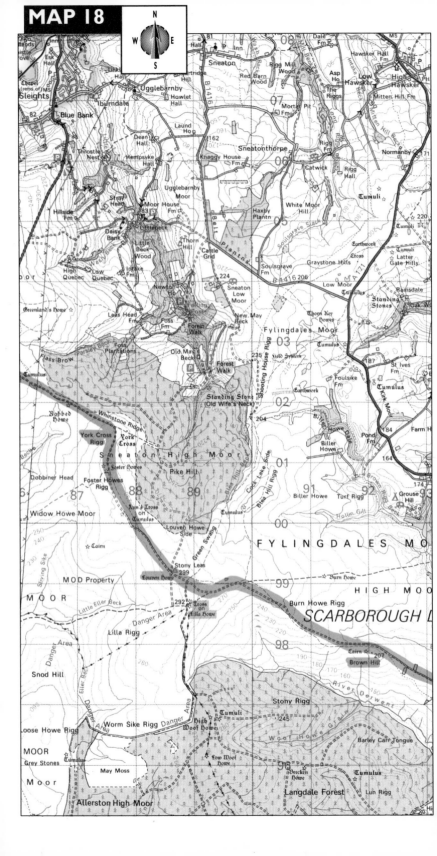

MAP 18

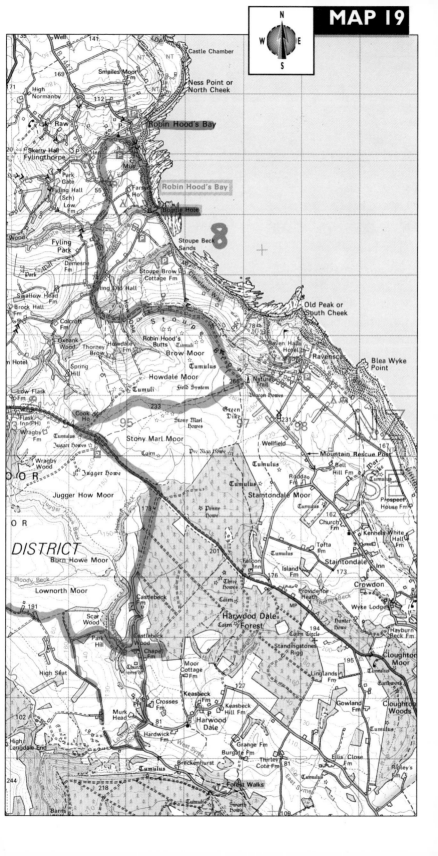

MAP 19

APPENDICES

The following pages are a directory of useful contacts for the Coast-to-Coast off-road cyclist including YHAs, bike shops, National Parks, National Trust, Forest Enterprise and Associations.

Weather News

Lake District in detail
Telephone: 05394 45151
(Normal rates)
Cumbria Weatherline
☎ 0891 500 419
The Dales Weatherline
☎ 0898 500 748
North-East England
Weatherline
☎ 0891 500 418

Youth Hostels Associations

Trevelyan House, 8 St Stephen's Hill, St Albans, Herts AL1 2DY
☎ 0727 855215
YHA Northern England Region for Camping Barn and Coast to Coast Walk information
☎ 0629 824571

Youth Hostels (En-route)

THE LAKE DISTRICT
Ennerdale ☎ 0946 861237
Black Sail Hut, Ennerdale
Eskdale ☎09467 23219
Coniston ☎ 05394 41323
Elterwater ☎ 09667 245
High Close, Langdale

☎ 09667 313
Ambleside ☎ 05394 32304
High Cross, Windermere
☎ 05394 43543

THE YORKSHIRE DALES
Kirkby Stephen
☎ 07683 71793
Keld ☎ 0748 86259
Grinton Lodge ☎ 0748 84202

THE NORTH YORKSHIRE MOORS
Osmotherley
☎ 0609 883575
Boggle Hole,Robin Hoods
☎0947 880352

Alternative Accommodation

SWALEDALE
Punchbowl Inn, Feetham
☎ 0748 86233

Bike Shops (En-route)

AMBLESIDE
Bike Treks, 2 Millans Park
☎ 05394 31245
Gyhllside Cycles , The Slack
☎ 05394 33592

RICHMOND
Arthur Caygill Cycles, Borough
Road, Gallowfields Trading
Estate ☎ 0748 825469

British Rail Booking Information

Carlisle ☎ 0748 825469
Darlington ☎ 091 232 6262

Tourist Information Centres

Whitehaven, Cumbria
☎ 0946 32582
Ambleside, Cumbria
☎ 05394 32582
Kirkby Stephen, Cumbria
☎ 07683 71199
Richmond, Yorkshire
☎ 0748 850252
Whitby, Yorkshire
☎ 0947 602674

National Park Offices

Lake District Nat Park,
Brockhole, Windermere,
Cumbria LA23 1LJ.
☎ 09662 6601
Yorkshire Dales Nat Park,
Colvend, Hebden Rd,
Grassington, Skipton, N Yorks
BD23 5LB. ☎ 0756 752748
**North Yorkshire Moors Nat
Park,** The Old Vicarage,
Bondgate, Helmsley, N Yorks
YO6 5BP. ☎ 0439 70657

Forest Enterprise Offices

Lakes Forest District,
Grizedale, Hawkshead,
Ambleside, Cumbria
LA22 0QJ. ☎ 0229 860373
**North Yorkshire Moors Forest
District**, 42 Eastgate,
Pickering, N Yorks YO18 7DU.
☎ 0751 72771

The National Trust

Cumbria - The Hollens,
Grasmere, Ambleside LA22
9QZ. ☎ 05394 35599
North Yorkshire - Goddards,
27 Tadcaster Road,
Dringhouses, York YO2 2QC.
☎ 0904 702021

County Council (Rights of Way)

**Cumbria - East Cumbria
Countryside Project,** The Old
Mill, Warwick Bridge, Carlisle
CA4 8RR. ☎ 0228 561601
**North Yorkshire - Surveyors
Dept., County Hall,**
Northallerton DL7 8AH.
☎ 0609 780780
North West Water Authority
Watchgate Water Treatment
Works, Kendal. ☎ 0539 83655

Further Reading

Practical First Aid, The British
Red Cross, Dorling Kindersley,
London 1991

The British Mountain Bike Federation

Since 1991 the BMBF has been the governing body for the sport of mountain biking in England and Wales and membership is open to anyone interested in mountain biking. Far from being a totally race-orientated organisation the BMBF carries out important work addressing access problems and promoting Rights of Way initiatives wherever they occur. This is done through a network of volunteer Access Officers. Those responsible for areas relevant to this ride are:

CUMBRIA

Andy Stephenson:
☎ 05394 31245
Jason Crellin:
☎ 0900 603419

YORKSHIRE DALES

Steve Chapman
☎ 0748 811855

N YORK MOORS

Graham Longstaff
☎ 0642 787844

Please remember that they are volunteers and carry out their BMBF duties without payment and in addition to their normal employment so contact them only if there is genuine need. If you would like to apply for membership then apply to: BMBF Memberships, 36 Rockingham Road, Kettering, Northants NN16 8HG.
☎ 0536 412211.

Benefits of being a member include:

- Representation on Rights of Way and access issues in your area.
- 3rd Party insurance cover up to £2M.
- Preferential bike and travel insurance rates.
- Free legal advice for cycling related problems.
- Free injury advice.
- Quarterly newsletter.
- A voice in the world of MTBing.

Author's Acknowledgements

The wardens and rangers of the Lake District, Yorkshire Dales and North Yorkshire Moors National Parks.

The BMBF Access Officers Andy Stevenson, Steve Chapman and Graham Longstaff and Andy Nicholson of ECCP for their invaluable advice.

The NNWA for permissive access on some of their service roads and finally, Ralph Coleman Cycles of Taunton for providing cycling clothes.